Weekday Ministry with Young Children

I saw tomorrow's children,
Through little children's eyes
And I thought how carefully we'd teach
If only we were wise.

—Author unknown

Weekday Ministry with Young Children

Martha Locke Hemphill

JUDSON PRESS, Valley Forge

WEEKDAY MINISTRY WITH YOUNG CHILDREN

Copyright © 1973
Judson Press, Valley Forge, Pa. 19481

Library of Congress Cataloging in Publication Data
Hemphill, Martha Locke.
    Weekday ministry with young children.
    Includes bibliographies.
    1. Religious education of preschool children.
I. Title.
[BV1475.7.H45]   268'.432   72-7594
ISBN 0-8170-0573-0

Contents

✵ 1 ✵
Why Teach?
The Ministry of Love

A certain style seemed to mark Jesus' relationships with other people:

- He did not judge nor evaluate others, except in special contexts.
- He encouraged cooperation rather than competition.
- He inspired self-confidence in others.
- He considered the feelings and fears of others.
- He respected children as persons.
- He had time for children's spontaneous curiosity.
- He knew that there is a certain quality of a child's spirit and attitude that once lost disqualifies a person from the really important aspects of life — even the kingdom of God.
- He was concerned with the "whole" person.
- He was aware of the crucial importance of human relationships in the development of persons.
- He knew that it is the young who carry in them the power to confirm those who confirm them.

There are many educators who believe that these very attitudes which we see in Jesus are also fundamental to real and significant education. Successful experimental schools have been developed on the basis of these convictions. The church believes that the most critical aspects of the learning situation are neither facilities nor equipment but the attitudes to which the child is exposed and the spirit of the relationships of which he becomes a part. But to what end? The purpose of education in the church is to enable each child to develop his full God-given potential, to be responsible, caring, creative, spontaneous, happy, and independent. In brief, the value of each child is affirmed and he is enabled, by means of the attitudes of the teachers and the conditions of the learning environment, to develop his full potential as a child of God.

The church, because it is dedicated to the attitudes and life-style exemplified by Jesus and is also designated as of fundamental importance by many contemporary educators, has the responsibility placed upon it and is qualified to provide those educational opportunities in which children can develop to their fullest potential.

Why should your church engage in this ministry with young children? To know that in your hands is the man or woman of tomorrow and to know that the best preparation for a child's tomorrow life is to live life fully right now may be a grave challenge, but where else can one feel so important, so necessary? Helping children become what they were created to be is truly being a fellow worker with God.

The attitudes of a child about himself, about others, and about his world are well formed by the time he starts first grade. How the child sees himself, his worth, his value, his uniqueness, his "somebodyness," all justify such a ministry. How the child sees others about him, their worth, their value, their uniqueness and "somebodyness" is important, too. Does he see the world as a friendly place? Does he feel his responsibility for himself, for others, and for his world? These are the seeds which need to be planted and nourished so that they will develop good strong roots and, in time, a full flowering.

We know that a child reaches his peak of creativity by age four and a half. Studies have shown a gradual decline in creativity as a child grows older. This loss of creativity is a man-made phenomenon. God, the great Creator, made us in his image. We are called to be creative. Creativity should not be stifled, no matter how hard it is to live with. There is a thought expressed in the UNESCO charter to the effect that wars begin in the minds of men. Someone else has said that the reason the history of mankind is such a wretched story is that there have never been enough creative, mature people at any one time in any one place. To nourish creative approaches in solving problems, whether they be in the area of conflict, language, art, or movement, then is one reason for the church to engage in this ministry.

In ministry with young children the qualities of loving, caring, forgiving, and accepting need to be foremost. The participial forms of the verbs are used to indicate the ongoingness of these qualities. Also within the meaning of ministry with young children are the qualities of openness, truth, courage, authenticity, and trustworthiness. It is a holy calling.

The scope of what the church has to offer in its work with young children is tremendous. The dimensions are as high as we are able to lift our sights and as wide as we will extend ourselves to live out God's love in relationships. As we live in loving, caring, forgiving, and accepting relationships with parents, children, and each other, we are ministering.

There are no more compelling reasons to engage in this ministry with young children than these: early childhood is the crucial time for this kind of learning, and our great commission is to "go and teach!"

Teaching requires a deep commitment to God and a desire to witness to his love. It requires a love and concern for children and the ability to relate to them. It requires a willingness to study the principles of early childhood learning and the methods of working with young children. It demands the third ear, the eye in the back of the head, and the empathy really to hear what a child is trying to say. A teacher must be willing to live and grow with the children and also to grow in self-understanding, in sensitivity to others and to one's surroundings.

These are the plus factors which the church has to offer. This is the *must* which churches will give, or else the church is being untrustworthy.

❊❊ 2 ❊❊
Is the Church Ready?
Telling the Good News

Are you, as a church, ready to sponsor a nursery school? Here they come, ready or not! Here's hoping you are ready for Eric and for Steve, for Cindy and for Linda. Church boards and commissions should examine themselves in order to determine whether they are trustworthy in offering this ministry to the young child.

Some denominations have suggested that the nursery school should have a priority rating in the program of Christian education of the local church. It might be wiser and also more honest if these programs were not thought of as "nursery school" but as ministry with the young child. Much of our untrustworthiness results from our confusing the church and its mission with the public school and its task.

Every discipline related to the psychology of education is stressing the importance of the early childhood years in the becoming of a person. The church, at its best, has always been concerned and aware of what happens in the lives of children, both at home and at church. Unfortunately, churches are not always at their best, and too few of them are aware of both the opportunities and the responsibilities which are theirs.

The focus is now on early childhood education, particularly in the Head Start and day care arenas. The primary concern of the government is for the economically deprived or the socially disadvantaged child, with the purpose of trying to prevent him from becoming a dropout or a potential liability to society.

Laudable as are these programs which have been initiated by the government and which are forcing our public schools to take a good look at themselves, the church is not relieved of its responsibility toward young children. Every child has a birthright which may be imperiled because of concepts formed during these early years about himself, others, and his world. Our responsibility is to enable him to become what he already is — God's own. This is our ministry to the young child and his family. Our opportunity is to live out the Good News moment by moment with him to insure that he will inherit the kingdom.

As we plan for this ministry, our challenge must be to tell

the Good News in every way possible, using every medium and relationship to convey it over and over. Teachers should think of themselves as mirrors in which each child sees himself as a person of worth. Relationships should convey the message of acceptance and forgiveness. Experiences should give each child feelings of adequacy and creativity. In order to do this we need to think of all the ways in which teaching-learning occurs with young children. How do young children learn? What does this say about our teaching?

Children learn through being — seeing, touching, hearing, tasting, and smelling.

Children learn through doing — playing, exploring, experiencing, experimenting, initiating, creating, and wondering.

Children learn through feelings — of being loved, of being adequate, of being valued, of being secure, of being accepted, and of being forgiven.

Our teaching must be based on these ways of learning. The objective of Christian education, interpreted at the nursery school level, can be stated as follows:

The Objective [1]	*The Interpretation*
The objective of the church's educational ministry is	Each teacher needs to have a clear understanding of why he or she is teaching in the church school, the importance of ministry in early childhood years, and what we are seeking to do.
that all persons	This ministry is for all persons; no child is excluded nor is his family. Every child needs to feel that he is wanted and loved.
be aware of God	God is known through others. God uses persons to make his love known. To lead young children to know God is to be the medium of his message to live in loving relationship with them.

[1] *Foundations for Curriculum* (Valley Forge: American Baptist Board of Education and Publication, 1966), p. 13.

through his self-disclosure

Children can know what God is like through the Bible. Stories of Jesus tell them that God cares for everyone. They know him through being loved.

especially his redeeming love as revealed in Jesus Christ,

They can know God's redeeming love through experiences of alienation and reconciliation. They learn that Jesus Christ is the center of our faith.

and enabled by the Holy Spirit

They know that they are not alone, that in experiences which are hard there is a power which enables them.

respond in faith and love; that as new persons in Christ

They learn that being open frees them to respond in ways of loving concern for others, that each day gives new opportunities to be caring persons,

they may know who they are and what their human situation means,

that they are unique, special, of worth — that they are able to *be,* and to help others *be,* that they have the responsibility of *being* and helping others *be.*

grow as sons of God rooted in the Christian community,

They learn that every day is important in becoming more Christian, that the church tries to help all people grow to Christian maturity — that all persons in the church are responsible for living as Christ in their relationships with one another.

live in obedience to the will of God in every relationship, fulfill their common vocation in the world,

Being responsible to God means living like Jesus in every relationship. It means that all persons are important in God's sight and therefore we should love one another.

and abide in Christian hope. Living in these ways all of our days is what God expects of us in doing our part to make his world what he wants it to be. At conference after conference in the fields of day care and early childhood education, speakers talk in such a vein that one would think he were attending a conference on Christian education. The burden of every message is that children need to hear the Good News. No, these are not the words used, but the import is there over and over. The importance of recognizing feelings of alienation or rejection and the necessity for feelings of acceptance and forgiveness, the acceptance of each child as an individual rather than fitting him into some researcher's data of what children are like, or should be like, is emphasized over and over. We actually have been encouraging little children to live lies by forcing them to put on masks to cover up feelings. "Little boys don't cry!" "Little girls must act nice!"

Persons responsible for publicity or interpreting the church nursery school program to outsiders need to be very familiar with the objectives for ministry with children. They need to guard against the clichés of *getting ready* for kindergarten or getting a *head start* on other children, and the emphasis, which is waning, on cognitive learning and the social adjustment pitfall. The above may be results of ministry but never the purpose.

Nursery school is not a prep school for kindergarten. Many people, however, have this narrow view because they do not understand the developmental tasks of the three-, four-, and five-year-olds, nor the learning process and the way God works through persons to effect Christian growth.

Public-school children are always being readied for the next grade. They are not free to live fully in the "right now." Classes are much too large and person-to-person relationships are virtually impossible. The schools have been likened to factories, the teachers to foremen, and the pupils to the product at the end of the assembly line. We hear teachers complaining about being painted into IQ corners and children being sacrificed on IQ crosses. In the church we maintain that each person is unique, a child of God, and he needs no programmed readiness to become what he already is. God will use teachers for his purposes if they are open to his leading.

❈ 3 ❈
How Shall We Begin?
Laying the Foundations

What procedures should be followed in a ministry with young children? Are there reliable guidelines to follow? Can a ministry such as this be self-supporting? Should it be part of the church budget? Who selects the teachers? These are some of the many questions which the congregation will ask.

There will be those church members who think the church should only be used by *their own*. There will also be those who think that the church should only be used on Sundays for such an experience. There will be those who fear that a nursery school will cost the church too much. There will be others who view a nursery school as a source of revenue and still others who will see the parents of these young children as potential church members. All of these positions have elements of truth in them.

To those who think the church is only for their own kind, the task is clear for interpreting the church in mission. For those who want the church used only on Sundays there will have to be the assurance that the teaching which will be done is a continuance of what should happen on Sunday. Should there be objections based on the fear that there will be more work involved, such as janitorial or secretarial help, again this is a valid concern and there should be recognition of this fact. There should be a budget allowance for these services. Good nursery school teachers leave their rooms clean and orderly. Often the same people involved in the weekday ministry are also involved in the Sunday ministry. As more nursery school groups are formed, a part-time secretary and a church matron (janitress), working three hours a day, may be hired. However, in the starting stages it might be well to increase the wages of the present staff to compensate them for the extra work.

A nursery or kindergarten room which has already been equipped for Sunday church school use, according to suggestions made by the denominational materials, should not cost too much and ought to pay its own way. If the room is not equipped, it will cost at least one thousand dollars a room to equip it. This amount will not vary too much.

In one church with a group of fifteen children enrolled, there was a deficit of eighty-five dollars at the end of the year. The only piece of equipment that was bought was a fireman's gym, at the cost of eighty-five dollars. This school now has a registration fee of twenty dollars per child or three hundred dollars a year for each group. There is now money on hand to make purchases of big pieces of equipment.

This same school, which is now in its fifteenth year of operation, has turned over to the church budget amounts averaging four thousand dollars a year for the past six years. At the present time it is paying seven thousand dollars into the church budget to cover half the custodial salaries and a third of the utilities and insurance.

This school has bought all of the equipment for a new building; materials for Sunday use also; a well-stocked library of books, tapes, films, and recordings for use by both parents and teachers; and the electronic equipment necessary for using the materials.

This school has made eighteen scholarships available to innercity children as well.

The following quote is from the front page of the parish paper of this church.

OUR WEEKDAY CHURCH SCHOOL AND THE DOXOLOGY

Our weekday Church School is cause for a hearty "Doxology"!

The enrollment of 303 children is in itself remarkable.

But even more impressive is the capable and dedicated staff of 20 teachers [serving these children].

But the most heartwarming aspect of all is the atmosphere provided by this Staff in which the children learn at their own pace about themselves, their world, and their relationships to others.

My impression is that each child in the school is considered and treated with the kind of dignity and respect that Jesus assumed every person deserved.

I like to think that the children in our Weekday Church School feel something of what the children felt the day Jesus turned from the adults to listen to them, and to let them know that they too belonged and counted.

You can't get much closer to the Kingdom of God than that!

At any rate, though it's hard for me to capture it in words, there's something tremendously important happening in our Weekday Church

School, and it's a fitting occasion for singing a humble but hearty "Doxology"![a]

The weekday ministry with young children should be under the supervision of a subcommittee of the Education Commission. Serving on this committee will be the Director of Children's Work (professional or nonprofessional), the Pastor or Minister of Education, and one or two persons who are acting out their concerns for young children. An equal number of parents of the children being served, preferably as many males as females, should also be represented on this committee. The parents do not necessarily have to be members of the church. The director of the Weekday School should also be on the committee, but only as a resource person. One of the duties of this committee is to hire those teachers who are needed and who have been recommended by the director.

Two teachers should be hired for each group of children to be enrolled. They need to work as a team, even though one may be more experienced than the other. Both are teachers! Salaries may be based upon experience, but togetherness in the classroom is the ideal, as it is for the parents in the home. Even though one teacher may be the school director, the other teacher and any parents who may be involved should feel their importance and value to the team effort.

Most schools offer a weekly two-day program for three-year-olds and a three-day program for four-year-olds. The optimum size group for threes should be at least fifteen for the first semester. Three, and no more than five, children and one more teacher may be added the second semester under some circumstances, the size of the room and the makeup of children's needs being determining forces. The class of four-year-olds should be limited to twenty children with two teachers. In the middle of the year, if circumstances are favorable, a few more children can be added to the group.

Many parents are not starting their children in public school kindergarten unless they are five years and six months old by September first. Some churches are offering a five-day-a-week group for such children. Group sizes are kept to twenty with two teachers.

[a] James S. Hook, "Our Weekday Church School and the 'Doxology,'" *The Parish Visitor* (October 4, 1967), published by the Crescent Avenue Church, 1232 Crescent Avenue, Fort Wayne, Indiana.

Another grouping which is becoming popular is one in which three-, four-, and five-year-olds are together in one group with three teachers. They are in a family grouping for routine activities but during free periods are in interest centers together. There is much to be said about the value of this kind of grouping if care is taken to protect each child's right to be where and what he is at the moment and not to be judged according to some group norm.

The weekday committee members should develop particulars for the school which cover enrollment, registration, tuition, schedules, parent conferences, transportation, and health regulations. They should develop a budget which includes salaries, acquisition of new equipment, maintenance of old equipment, and purchase of raw materials and snacks. They should also provide for subsidizing the school during the first year, if it is necessary.

The weekday operation should be part of the church budget. All income should go into the church treasury, and disbursements should be made from it.

A realistic budget on which a church can operate a group of twenty four-year-olds three days a week follows. Tuition of $20 a month would be charged, plus a preregistration fee of $20, payable upon application for enrollment. Two teachers would be needed and a sliding pay scale adopted, ranging from $6.50 to $10.50 per morning or $17 per session. There should be an allowance of $1.25 per child per month for materials — paper, paints, snacks, and such. Yearly income and outgo for a group of twenty for three days a week would break down like this:

Income		Expenses	
Preregistration fees	$ 400.00	Salaries	$1836.00
Tuition	$3600.00	Expendable materials	$ 250.00
Total	$4000.00	Total	$2086.00

For a two-day-a-week program for three-year-olds in a group of fifteen, tuition is $15 a month and the preregistration fee is $20. The budget looks like this:

Income		Expenses	
Preregistration fees	$ 300.00	Salaries	$1224.00
Tuition	$2025.00	Materials	$ 168.75
Total	$2325.00	Total	$1392.75

The church picks up its part of the deduction for social security, and of course salaries could be higher. However, if teachers are motivated by salary only, the concept of ministry to the family breaks down. As the school grows and more groups are added, there will be more money to hire personnel for administration, janitorial and special services, such as consultants in early childhood, mental health, and the like. Provision must be made to underwrite on-the-job training expenses for teachers, too, such as fees for lectures, labs, and so on.

The weekday committee should decide whether it can make scholarships available for needy children. Parents should be made aware of federal income tax deductions which may be made for child care if both parents are working or going to school.

There is a possibility that your school can be reimbursed by your state at a fixed rate per lunch.

The church should not become involved in the transportation of the children. This is one of the responsibilities of your parent groups. The church may tack on a bulletin board a map of the area being served. As each registration comes in, a pin can be placed at the spot where the child resides. Should it be an apartment complex or housing development, use color coding to indicate the number of children involved. The parents of the children then assume responsibility both for contact and for the formation of car pools. The church only assumes the responsibility to get parents in touch with one another by offering information or by holding a meeting for this purpose before school starts.

No child should be excluded from nursery school if your church is truly ministering. As long as there is room, more and more groups can be formed. This may require staggering playground facilities, but it can be done so that the child never has the feeling of being swallowed up by bigness. Children who require a structured situation to feel secure can be in small groups for a part of a morning. If they are stimulated by too much freedom, they may stay for only an hour or so. Blind children, deaf children, and mentally retarded children, as well as so-called normal children, do minister to one another. Even in places where there are special schools for handicapped young children, these schools are now asking nursery schools to accept their children for a few hours a week on a ratio of one handicapped child to an average-size group of so-called normal children.

⚜ 4 ⚜
If You Can Answer "Yes"
Making Our Commitment

The following guidelines have been developed to enable churches to determine whether they are ready to sponsor and establish a nursery school.

1. Do you have mature, experienced leaders who are sensitive to children's needs, abilities, and feelings? One of these teachers should have fulfilled minimum academic requirements for public school teaching and in addition must be fully in sympathy with your objectives in Christian education for the young child. The teachers must recognize the importance of parent-teacher-child-church relationships and be able, willing, and happy to work in these relationships. At least one of the leaders should be recognized by and associated with the existing agencies in the community which relate themselves to child guidance and welfare.

2. Can you provide a program which maintains a happy, relaxed atmosphere at all times, balancing interesting activities with adequate rest? The program needs to be flexible enough to keep a child from feeling pressured, yet with enough routine to give the child a sense of orderliness. The activities, very carefully chosen, must be challenging and significant for spiritual growth in all areas of Christian education. In addition, the teacher will be alert to the individual needs of each child and will plan experiences which will help him. For example, a child who has a feeling that he can't do things may be helped to a better feeling about himself by being given opportunities to succeed.

3. Can you provide the kind and amount of room space and the kind of equipment young children need, and keep to the standards for adult-child ratio and group size? [3]

[3] See the following: "Some Ways of Distinguishing a Good School for Young Children," National Association for the Education of Young Children; Helen Burgess, "How to Choose a Nursery School," *Public Affairs Pamphlet*, no. 310, March, 1961; James Hymnes, "Three to Six: Your Child Starts to School," *Public Affairs Pamphlet*, no. 163, 2nd edition, April, 1965.

4. Can you provide an outdoor play area with equipment for large muscle play and climbing, sandbox and digging space, saw horses, planks, barrels, outdoor easels, and workbenches? This space must be safe and enclosed. Many churches are using snow fencing for this purpose; it is less expensive than many other types of fencing and is quite satisfactory. Do not minimize the importance of this area, as some of your most important teaching-learning will go on here. Some of your church people may consider this play area unsightly, and you will need to be ready to answer their objections.

5. Is your school under the supervision of an advisory board responsible to the board of Christian education and closely related to the Sunday morning program for three- and four-year-olds in your church? On this advisory board there must be parent representation.

6. Has the advisory board developed particulars for your school which cover personnel policies and teacher responsibilities?

7. Has the advisory board developed particulars which cover enrollment, registration, tuition, schedules, parent conferences, transportation, and health regulations? Enrollment particulars should cover ages of children to be admitted and procedures for making application. Registration should cover responsibilities of parents to *participate fully* as a prerequisite to their child being accepted officially. The tuition particulars should state not only the fee, but also how and when it is to be paid. The procedures to be followed, tuition wise, in case of illness or extended absence should be determined. It is necessary to make a policy regarding this situation and abide by it except in case of hardship. The schedule should include school hours, times of arrival and departure, days of the week, and the yearly calendar. Many schools have found a satisfactory schedule which provides two weekday mornings for three-year-olds and three mornings for four-year-olds, in addition to the Sunday morning hours. The extent of parent responsibility for transportation and times for observation and conferences should be outlined. Health certificates for both teachers and children should be required, with chest X-rays in addition for the teachers.

The particulars should also include policies to be followed in case of unexpected illness while the child is at school.

8. Have you developed a budget for your school which includes salaries, acquiring new equipment, maintaining old equipment, purchasing raw materials and midmorning snacks? Most churches find that they have to subsidize a school, particularly during the first year.

9. Have you investigated the insurance angles which affect you and the children while in the church or on the playground? Most churches carry a blanket-type of insurance which protects the church as well as individuals in the church building.

10. Have you made a survey of your church and the community not only to determine the need for such a school but also to ascertain the actual enrollment on which you can count? Most churches report that only a third of their enrollment comes from church-related homes. In the talking stage, however, they were led to believe that the enrollment would be much higher. It has also been a fact that many inactive church homes in the community have been revitalized and the families have related themselves anew to their own church or have brought their membership to the sponsoring church.

11. Have you complied with all regulations set down by your State Department of Public Instruction and Department of Public Welfare? In areas where there are local regulations, have you complied with them, too?

If you have not done these things, do not start such a church nursery school. Recently, in one midwestern city three schools closed while other schools had long waiting lists. Unfortunately some of the schools which have had to close were probably better than some of the existing ones. They started, however, before they were thoroughly ready.

While you are getting ready for such a venture, do these things:

1. Start a publicity campaign for better nursery schools. Make the public aware of the standards for good nursery education. Challenge some of the obsolete requirements of local and state regulations.

2. Send your prospective teachers to lab schools sponsored by your denomination and also to personal growth labs.
3. Read widely in the field of early childhood education. Become aware of programs in parent education. Join the National Association for the Education of Young Children, 1834 Connecticut Ave., N.W., Washington, D.C. 20009.

❆❆ 5 ❆❆
Off to a Good Start
Embarking upon the Adventure

Starting a weekday nursery school after you are ready can be one of the most satisfying adventures your church has ever embarked upon. As one pastor said recently, "If you want to witness life-changing experiences, you ought to drop in some time and silently observe the weekday nursery in session. These children have such individual attention that it makes one wonder why anyone would hesitate to send his child. One thing I am sure of — when these children get older, the church will not be a strange building to them. They feel as much at home in the church as, we hope, they learn to feel with God, himself."

The teachers feel rewarded by the association with the children — their simple relationships, their frankness and honesty. The parents become aware of the importance of these early years in the lives of their children and are thankful for the opportunities given them by the church in the way of specific helps and insights. They report that a new quality is added to their children's lives, their activities, and their faith.

The children will know their church as a good place to be. They will know the adults there as their friends. They will learn the most important things about themselves, others, and their world at the time they can best learn them.

What are some of the procedures which will help you to get off to a good start? Publicity? Yes, with the foci on the church's ministry to young children as the concern and the reason for starting the venture.

For the last few years it has not been necessary to have any publicity campaigns before opening a nursery school or day-care center. Sending your child to nursery school is now the "in" thing to do. IBM (I've Been Moved) families check out the availability of schools before leaving their old communities. It is not unusual for some nursery schools to have long distance phone calls from far away requesting application forms. Those individuals who are distressed by the caliber of some of these church-sponsored nursery schools can do very little as the demand is so great. Parents usually do not shop for a nursery school by pacing off floor space, counting toilets, and inspecting play facilities. There are just not enough nursery schools, and the concern is more with getting in than with the adequacy of the facilities.

The nursery and kindergarten materials published by your church headquarters include guidelines for space, optimum size of groups, child-adult ratio, and program. They should be considered as guidelines, however, and not as blueprints to be followed to the letter. Since most state regulations and church guidelines stress first-floor or ground-level rooms, one church was apprehensive when it grew so large that more rooms had to be made available on the second floor. This proved to be a plus factor, however. Children need to climb up and go down stairs. It is a very important developmental task which many children living in one-story homes do not have the opportunity to perform. Children with motor perceptual difficulties can be spotted if carefully observed while performing this task. For either a three- or a four-year-old there is a tremendous sense of achievement when he arrives on his own at the top or the bottom of a staircase.

Parents do need to be concerned about the philosophy of the program and the emotional climate of the rooms. Dr. Fritz Redl, while speaking one time about Russian nursery schools, said that they were good and bad just as in the United States. He said that you could smell a good nursery school. One may not be able to use the olfactory process, but he can certainly sense a good or bad situation.

Parents should visit a school before enrolling a child and should be able to answer "yes" to the following statements:

1. Children move freely about the playroom and playground.
2. Children select and use materials without adult interference.
3. Children may spend as much time as they choose to complete their work or play.
4. Materials and equipment are always put away by the children if they have finished with them.
5. The teacher often sits near an activity without entering into it, indirectly encouraging and facilitating play.
6. Adults talk and listen to a child on a face-to-face level.
7. When children speak, offer ideas, contribute suggestions, share an experience, etc., adults listen to them.

8. The teacher positively acknowledges children's contributions whether they are ideas, suggestions, experiences, or actions.
9. The teacher and other adults speak to the child in positive language.
10. The teacher and other adults freely give praise for each child's efforts.
11. Children initiate ideas and plans for work and play, and adults are available to help the children carry them out.
12. Materials and equipment for the children's use are where children can see them and where children can help themselves to them.

Parents should be able to answer "no" to the following:

1. All children engage in the same activity at the same time.
2. Children are expected to join and remain with a group activity which is directed by the teacher.
3. Children's activities are interrupted when the clock says it is time for the next scheduled activity.
4. Group activities are encouraged more than individual activities.
5. Loud and boisterous play is prohibited at all times.
6. Sharing materials, regardless of the child, situation, or experience, is required by the teachers.
7. The teachers tell children what to do.
8. Children are required to walk in line when moving from place to place.
9. Children speak only when given permission.
10. Children wait for teacher instructions and patterns before constructing their own products.
11. Children's requests, wishes, or desires are ignored.
12. The schedule of the day's events or plans is rigidly adhered to.

Again, these principles should only serve as a guideline. Both parents and teachers should realize that circumstances may change a "yes" to a "no," or vice versa, and that flexibility is necessary.

In one community the associated churches — including Catholics, Jews, Fundamentalists, and main line Protestants — persuaded a regional campus of their state university to offer a seminar in nursery education to all of the churches in the area which were offering or were contemplating offering nursery schools in the fall. This experience led to three or more seminars of eighteen hours each being offered every year. An Early Childhood Association grew out of this group experience and became affiliated with the national organization. This relationship enabled the churches to bring top-level people as speakers to the area.

The need for this kind of training is shown by the following situation. In the very first meeting of this seminar, not one of the buzz groups came up with any very good reasons why churches should offer this ministry, nor did any of the participants know the goals of Christian education at the nursery level. The importance of the early years for building positive attitudes toward oneself and others was not even mentioned. The seminar helped everyone to evaluate his own situation, and all agreed it was long overdue.

❈❈ 6 ❈❈
Who Shall Teach?
The One with the Light Touch

One, two, three for you, teacher! I've found you! You're it!

Who is this qualified teacher? What must this person bring to a teaching-learning situation? Where do the philosophies of ministry to the young child and of teaching the public school child differ? Is becoming what one already is the same thing as a readiness program? Are methods and techniques for handling groups of children to be equated with the Christian experience of living with children in ways which help them to experience the good news about themselves, others, and their world?

Far too often the church which is getting ready to offer a weekday learning situation for young children begins its search for a teacher by looking for someone with a degree in elementary or secondary education. This fact is ironical since the public school system has operated on the principle that formal learning does not take place, as a result of teaching, until the child has passed his fifth birthday. It shows how far afield from ministry many church-sponsored schools may be.

At the Citizen's Conference on Priorities and Action for Children and Youth in Washington, D.C. (Dec. 2-4, 1971), Dr. Vito Perrone said that there would have to be changes made in licensing requirements for teachers. He spoke of the need to bring creative people into the classroom. He is quoted as saying, "The laws now don't protect the child from incompetent teachers. The laws don't guarantee a good education to the child. They keep out the most competent people." [4]

In a paragraph in *Behavior Today*, the Office of Child Development, looking beyond political bickering over day care, is concerned about staffing:

"BA's? We'll never produce enough of them," OCD director Edward Zigler concludes. So early next year the agency will launch a new child care profession—the child development associate. Zigler says associates will be certified by competence, not by degree. He's now choosing professional child worker associations to do the certifying in institutions and

[4] "Perrone Advises Teachers to Shift Attention," *Report on Preschool Education*, December 29, 1971, p. 7.

in the field. For info contact Jenny Klein, Project Head Start, P.O. Box 1182, Wash., D.C. 20013.[5]

Only 1,200 teachers prepared to work at the early childhood ("preschool") level were graduated from American colleges in 1968. Few states have training programs for paraprofessionals in this field. Few states have certification requirements for "preschool" personnel. In 1967, only six states had special certificates for nursery school and kindergarten teachers and only five had a special endorsement on elementary certificates.[6]

The following quotes are also taken from the *Preliminary Report of the Ad Hoc Joint Committee on the Preparation of Nursery and Kindergarten Teachers* of the National Education Association. "The concept of teacher certification is in a state of flux. There is a growing trend among the states toward reviewing existing regulations for all educational personnel and for improving and 'liberalizing' standards and procedures." [7] The final paragraph in the report reads:

> The committee believes that certification or licensure cannot be based solely on the number of credits collected. We hope that states will move quickly in the direction of evaluation of competence as the basis for initial certification or licensure and for subsequent professional advancement at all levels of education, not only in early childhood education.[8]

The United Methodist Church in Indiana has set up three learning lab stations and a program of certification at different levels on a continuum whereby beginners can move on to more advanced levels.

There are few teachers who have the master's degree in early childhood education as there are still all too few institutions training them. These people are needed for college teaching and on-the-job supervision, such as agency directors, consultants to schools, communities, and early childhood centers. A church-sponsored school cannot afford experts except on a consultation basis. If the 4C's program (Community Coordinated Child Care) becomes a reality in your community, we hope it will be able to provide the kind of coordination of services that will make consultants a reality, too.

[5] "Day Care Parapros," *Behavior Today*, vol. 2, no. 48 (November 29, 1971), p. 2.

[6] Martin Haberman and Blanche Persky, eds., *Preliminary Report of the Ad Hoc Joint Committee on the Preparation of Nursery and Kindergarten Teachers*, published by the National Education Association, p. 6.

[7] *Ibid.*, p. 19.

[8] *Ibid.*, p. 23.

Write to the Department of Public Instruction in your state for requirements on certification of teachers. Most states do not require certification of nursery school teachers as so many parents are being used as paraprofessionals now in order to comply with government guidelines. (On February 20, 1972, the state legislature of Indiana passed a law exempting church nursery schools from licensing requirements.)

You will also need to write to the Department of Health and Welfare in your state for regulations on physical health and safety in schools. A common rule is that teachers must have chest x-rays taken every two years and that the results must be negative. In addition, the church must be sure that teachers are in good physical and emotional health. As for the building, there is usually no check of it if lunches are not being served. However, heating, ventilation, and lighting should all be carefully checked, as well as all fire safety provisions. Your church will need to comply with all state and local regulations if you do not already do so.

Some in-service training courses which may be made available by the church to teachers might include subjects such as these: Creating a Nurturing Environment, Teacher-Child Relationships, The Child in the Family, Children's Literature, Art and Music, Child and Family and Community, Working with Parents, Self-understanding, The Role of Play in Cognitive Learning, and any others which enhance awareness or sensitivity in personal growth.

What kind of persons will these teachers be to whom parents will be entrusting their children? These persons must be growing, continually searching, experimenting, reading, and learning ways of becoming better carriers of the *good news* to the children, their parents, and to their co-workers. These persons can never be static nor content with what they have learned in the past about teaching methods and techniques.

Many exciting things are happening in the field of education today. There is a recognition of the relationship between feelings and learning. Currently there is a redirection of methodology to let children discover things for themselves. There is also a growing awareness of the importance of person-oriented teaching as opposed to things-teaching and a recognition that the teaching of meanings and significance is more important than the teaching of facts. We who have been teaching in our church schools recognize these changes as reflective of the way the Master Teacher taught. A church which chooses teachers only upon the basis of their having completed some academic work done in the past, in either the elementary field or secondary education field, will find that these persons will have much to unlearn.

There are other factors which qualify a teacher for ministry with young children that are far more important than those which would legislate certification. Fortunately, at all levels of school and state governments we are beginning to challenge some of the old practices.

These teachers must be mature enough to have accepted fully themselves as persons whom God is using for his purposes. It will then follow that they will accept the children as they are, will be aware of the importance of feelings — theirs and the children's — and will not seek to dominate or manipulate others. They will be aware that the curriculum will encompass what is happening in the lives and experiences of the children, both at home and at church. The measuring stick for evaluating these experiences will be the number of times each child experiences good news about himself out of his relationships.

Ideal teachers are the ones with the *light touch*. They have been helped, are being helped, or are growing in awareness of themselves, their realness, and their value, to the end that they are not anxious about themselves as persons nor about risking themselves in relationships with other teachers, parents, or children. They are becoming free from the fear of not measuring up to someone else's standards for themselves as they know themselves, or are beginning to know themselves and to understand their own feelings. They sit loosely on themselves with the result that they are not uptight about themselves. They do not judge themselves harshly. Unimportant things remain that way rather than getting blown up out of all proportion to the real ministry which they are performing. They trust themselves and their ability to live with others in such a way that they enable others to know themselves, too, in the same way that they have been helped. They free persons they come in contact with to live in the same way with others.

Teachers with the light touch do not have to control others, either as a group or as individuals, because they know that each person has to do his own growing. Their teaching is not manipulative but rather *affirmative* of each person's ability to find the answers to his own questions by an inner motivation.

Teachers with the light touch are not slaves to the curriculum, the schedule, or the patterns of a typical day, since they are so well aware that the kind of learning which has meaning cannot fit into little boxes of time or materials.

Teachers with the light touch do not tack labels on behavior as naughty, immature, or nice, nor on performance as right or wrong. They do not presume to be judges but rather perform a band-aid ministry to the hurt place a child is showing by his behavior.

Teachers with the light touch do not consider their teaching as jobs with which they have been stuck. They feel that it is a real privilege to live in the here-and-now relationships with children and their families. They have experienced the truth of losing themselves and finding fulfillment in these relationships. They know the joy of being recognized as trustworthy.

Teachers with the light touch are not wordy; they listen. They know that they can tell someone, without saying a word, that he is special, that they are glad he is here, that he can act responsibly. They also know the value of the restraining touch when a child's controls are weak and he is crying for help by his behavior.

Teachers with the light touch know the value of play. They move about quietly, realizing that play is the sincerest expression of what is in a child's soul. They permit a child to feel alienation but never allow him to feel it without working through to some kind of reconciliation — no crucifixions without resurrections!

Where do we look for such teachers? One place may be within your own church school. There you may find persons living out their concerns for young children by volunteering their Sunday mornings, by taking lab schools, and by reading in the fields of early childhood psychology. These are the growing people. They may or may not have a degree in education. Certainly they do not need to be defensive about the lack of one. However, they must be professional in their attitudes. Study in the fields of child development and human relations, nursery and child-care programs, and community programs which have services related to child nurture — all should be part of the in-service training of teachers.

Listed below are sample questions which might be asked prospective teachers:

1. What would you hope to achieve with three-year-olds? What are your goals?
2. What would you hope to achieve with four-year-olds? What are your goals?
3. How do you think the content of nursery school teaching should differ from that of kindergarten?
4. How would you describe an ideal nursery school teacher?
5. How do you think three-year-olds learn?
6. How do you think four-year-olds learn?
7. What kinds of art experiences would you consider appropriate for three-year-olds? for four-year-olds?
8. What experiences would you like to provide in music with three-year-olds? with four-year-olds?
9. How do you feel about play? How much of the two-and-a-half-hour morning would you use for play?
10. What activities would you do as a group rather than individually? with three-year-olds? with four-year-olds? Do you think all children should participate in a group activity? What is the maximum amount of time you feel that nursery children should sit still?
11. How do you feel about noise?
12. What kind of problem would you consider serious in a child? What signs would alert you?
13. Are you familiar with the use of interest centers?
14. How would you feel about visiting other schools, attending teachers' meetings, using professional consultation from an experienced teacher, or attending a learning lab?
15. Are you acquainted with the nursery and curriculum materials of our denomination?

At the 1970 conference in Boston of the National Association for the Education of Young Children, Dr. Edward Zigler said that we need to develop a cadre of workers very much like those we find in other nations, but that have no counterpart in this country. We do have and have had for many years their counterpart in our church schools. He spoke of establishing courses to develop the new type of child-care worker with the training going on in the centers themselves. We have been doing this in our churches for years. We have recognized that every parent is a teacher and that children learn from them.

❀ 7 ❀
We Need to Know
Who Is the Child?

Your church nursery school will need to have an information sheet to send to all interested parents, giving the complete information pertaining to the school, regarding schedules, registration, tuition, and all requirements. It should tell parents anything which they might wish to know about the school before deciding to enroll their child in your program. Your information sheet might look like this:

The Weekday Nursery School at _____ Church is a school that operates five days a week under the supervision of the Commission on Christian Education of the _____ Church, and under the direction of the Children's Work Council of that Commission.

The school operates in five divisions:
1. Three-Year-Olds Div.* — Tues. & Thurs. mornings — 15.00 per month
2. Four-Year-Olds Div.** — Tues. & Thurs. afternoons — 15.00 per month
3. Four-Year-Olds Div.** — Mon., Wed., Fri. mornings — 20.00 per month
4. Four-Year-Olds Div.** — Mon., Wed., Fri. afternoons — 20.00 per month
5. Fours & Fives Div. — Mon. through Fri. morns. — 30.00 per month

REGISTRATION: A fee of $20 is charged with the registration of each child and is for the purpose of securing a place in the school. If there are two children enrolled from the same family, the registration fee is $35 for both children. A subscription to *Today's Child* is also included as part of the registration fee. No child is enrolled before this fee is paid, and it covers the insurance for each child. Half of the registration fee is refundable if we are notified of the child's withdrawal two weeks prior to school's opening.

TUITION: Tuition for the nursery school is payable monthly. Payment is due *in advance* on the first of each month. The tuition for Monday, Wednesday, and Friday is $20 per month; for Tuesday and Thursday the tuition is $15 per month. In the case of families where there are two children enrolled, the tuition rate is $24.50 for Tuesday and Thursday for both children and $34.50 for Monday, Wednesday, and Friday for both children. If one child comes on Tuesday and Thursday and the other on Monday, Wednesday, and Friday, the tuition for both children is $30.

One week's grace is allowed for payment, and a penalty of two dollars is added thereafter. There will be no refunds in case of absence, and two weeks' notice must be given in case of withdrawal. Checks are to be made payable to "_____ Church" and mailed c/o _____, administrative secretary of the school. In case of weather emergencies, we close if public schools are closed—tuition not refunded. Listen to your radio for school closings. Do not call the church.

HEALTH: Child should have or have started immunizations for diphtheria, measles, polio, and tetanus before being admitted to the nursery school. We have registered nurses on our staff, and children will be given first aid in case of accidents. Further medical treatment is the responsibility of the parent.

SCHEDULE: The scheduled morning for the nursery school begins at 9:00 and ends at 11:30 o'clock. Children are to be called for at 11:30 and are not to arrive before 8:45 A.M. The scheduled afternoon is from 1:00 to 3:30 o'clock. Children are to be called for at 3:30 and are not to arrive before 12:50.

TELEPHONE: If necessary to call the church, the number is _____.

If there should be days when school is canceled to conform with the public school schedule (*weather only exception*), parents will be notified in advance.

The first day of school for the Monday, Wednesday, Friday group is September ___; for the Tuesday, Thursday group it is September ___.

PARENTS ONLY Orientation for the Mon., Wed., Fri. groups—Wed., Sept. ___, 8:00 P.M.

PARENTS ONLY Orientation for the Tues., Thurs. groups—Thurs., Sept. ___, 8:00 P.M.

OPEN HOUSE for the Tues., Thurs. morning groups, children and parents— Sept. ___, 9:00-11:30 A.M.

OPEN HOUSE for the Tues., Thurs. afternoon groups, children and parents— Sept. ___, 1:00-3:30 P.M.

OPEN HOUSE for the Mon., Wed., Fri. morning groups, children and parents— Sept. ___, 9:00-11:30 A.M.

OPEN HOUSE for the Mon., Wed., Fri. afternoon groups, children and parents —Sept. ___, 1:00-3:30 P.M.

VACATION SCHEDULES: (Opening dates of school—Sept. ___)

    Veterans' Day
    Teachers' Institute
    Thanksgiving
    Christmas
    Easter
    Last day of school

* Children who will start public school in the fall of _____.
** Children who will start public school in the fall of _____.

Once the parents have decided to enroll their child in your school, they will need to fill out a registration form, giving you as much information as they can about their child so that it will enable you to be of the greatest help to him that you can. It will aid you to know the child's needs and interests as fully as possible. The registration sheet could take the following format:

CHILD'S NAME _____ BIRTH DATE _____

HOME ADDRESS _____ TELEPHONE _____

FATHER'S NAME _____ OCCUPATION _____ CHURCH _____

MOTHER'S NAME _____ OCCUPATION _____ CHURCH _____

PEOPLE IN THE HOME: Father _____ Mother _____ Ages and sex of older children _____

Ages and sex of younger children _____

Other adults in home _____

Is mother employed? _____ If so, in whose care is the child while she is gone? _____

Is this an adopted child? _____ Age at time of adoption _____

PHYSICALLY

What play materials or equipment seem to hold his attention the longest? (Both indoor and outdoor):

Is there some special health condition about which we should know? (For instance, are there any activities which should be avoided?) _____

At what age did he walk? _____ Is your child right- or left-handed? _____

Have you any reason to suspect hearing loss? _____

Is there anything significant which we should know that might affect your child's physical or emotional well-being? _____

INTELLECTUALLY

Is your child particularly interested in books? _____

What subjects does he ask questions about? _____

What are his special interests? _____

SOCIALLY

About how much time does he spend watching TV? _____

About how much waking time each day does he usually spend alone, excluding TV watching? _____

With other children? _____

Age of playmates? _____ Is he more at home with adults or children? _____ In what kind of situation will your child need the most help? _____

EMOTIONALLY

Do you feel that you have discipline difficulties with your child? _____

How do you try to handle or avoid them? _____

Are you aware of fears or anxieties your child has? If so, what? _____

Does he find it difficult or easy to share possessions with others? _____

Check which ones best describe your child: confident ___ insecure ___ trusting ___ hostile ___ rebellious ___ anxious ___ responsible ___ self-reliant ___ leader ___ follower ___ cooperative ___ loving ___ fearful ___

TO BE ANSWERED BY BOTH PARENTS: What do you enjoy most about your child?

_____

_____

_____

_____

_____

Division preferred (see particulars). First choice _____

TO BE FILLED IN BY CHURCH STAFF:
Date application received _____
Date registration fee paid _____
Group in which child is placed _____

As a school, there are two more forms that you will require a parent to fill out. One is the form which deals with the information you need about the child in case of a sudden illness or a serious accident in school. It might be worded in this way:

DATE _____ FULL NAME OF CHILD _____
AGE _____ DATE OF BIRTH _____
HOME ADDRESS _____ HOME PHONE _____
NAME OF FATHER _____ WHERE EMPLOYED _____
BUSINESS PHONE _____ OCCUPATION _____
NAME OF NEIGHBOR OR CLOSE RELATIVE _____ PHONE _____

Dear Parents,

Our procedure in cases of emergency, such as sudden illness or serious accidents, is: (1) to render first aid; (2) to contact home immediately for instructions as to: transportation to home, doctor to be called, and hospital acceptable.

In some cases, failure to establish contact with either parent has delayed treatment.

DOCTOR _____ PHONE _____
HOSPITAL PREFERENCE _____

Only after all reasonable efforts have been made to contact you, will we call your doctor, and only in the most extreme cases will your child be taken to the hospital.

YOU HAVE MY PERMISSION TO ACT ACCORDINGLY.

(Please sign) _____

The other form is called the "blanket permission" form in which the parent agrees to allow his child to be taken on any field trips. The blanket permission form may be worded thus:

BLANKET PERMISSION

_____ has my permission to go on any field trip which has been scheduled by either the nursery school or the day-care center. I understand that I will be notified in advance of any such trips* and that special insurance is taken out for every such excursion. If bus fare or fees are involved, I am responsible; and if on the date of the trip some circumstance should arise that my child cannot go, I understand that there will be no school that day and I will keep him at home.

Signed _____

* Walking trips in the area excepted.

8
Before School Starts
Getting Ready

There should be school visitations the week before school starts. This enables each child, accompanied by one or both parents, to meet the teachers and also to get acquainted with his schoolroom surroundings. It is a good idea to make this a festive occasion with a punch bowl of juice and cookies. Parents may fill out health and permission slips at this time, and the child picks up the name tag which he will wear the first week of school. Samples of open-house particulars from a large school follow:

Dear Parents,

We are holding a series of coffees on Monday mornings at 9:15 in the Youth Lounge for the purpose of acquainting parents with some of the many facets of our program, to answer individual questions, and to allow some room visitation.

Your morning to visit is _____, and we will expect you unless we hear differently from you.

Most sincerely,

_____, Director
Weekday Nursery School

TO: The Parents of our Weekday Nursery School Children:

Note Carefully

OPEN HOUSE is, as the term implies, an in-and-out situation. Children are expected anytime between the hours and on only one of the days listed. There has been confusion about this in the past. The purpose of this experience is for the child and parents to get acquainted with the room and teachers.

MONDAY, WEDNESDAY, FRIDAY MORNING GROUPS* (School starts officially Sept. ___)

Parent Orientation—Wed., Sept. ___, 8:00 P.M.

OPEN HOUSE for children and mothers—Wed., Sept. ___, 9:00-11:30 A.M.

September tuition—$15, payable Sept. 1.

MONDAY, WEDNESDAY, FRIDAY AFTERNOON GROUPS* (School starts officially Sept. ___)

Parent Orientation—Wed., Sept. ___, 8:00 P.M.

OPEN HOUSE for children and mothers—(one day only), Wed., Sept. ___, 1:00-3:30 P.M.

September tuition—$15, payable Sept. 1.

TUESDAY AND THURSDAY MORNING GROUPS* (School starts officially Sept. ___)

Parent Orientation—Thurs., Sept. ___, 8:00 P.M.

OPEN HOUSE for children and mothers—Tues., Sept. ___, 9:00-11:30 A.M.
or   Thurs., Sept. ___, 9:00-11:30 A.M.

September tuition—$10, payable Sept. 1.

TUESDAY AND THURSDAY AFTERNOON GROUPS* (School starts officially Sept. ___)

Parent Orientation—Thurs., Sept. ___, 8:00 P.M.

OPEN HOUSE for children and mothers—(one day only), Tues., Sept. ___, 1:00-3:30 P.M.

September tuition—$10, payable Sept. 1.

* One or both parents must attend Parent Orientation. You will need to know in which group your child has been placed, meet the teachers and staff in the school, form car pools and be assigned car pool numbers, pick up your child's name tag if he hasn't already done so at the OPEN HOUSE. The difference between a good start for your child and a confusing one depends on how well the mechanics of orientation have been resolved.

_____ has been placed in Group _____ which will meet in Room _____ on days _____.

Sincerely yours,

Director, Weekday Nursery School

There needs to be an orientation meeting of all parents one evening before school starts. This is the time to focus on their importance in the school, their suggestions, and their involvement. Let them know that what their child brings from his home background is one of your richest curriculum resources.

One good way to open the meeting is to use the following litany. This litany was suggested by one which was used by Jesse Jackson in the Chicago *Operation Breadbasket*.

People repeat what the leader says, using the same rhythm and intonation.

LEADER: I may be overly conscientious—but—I am SOMEBODY!
People repeat.
LEADER: I may make mistakes—*but* I am SOMEBODY!
People repeat.
LEADER: I may be anxious—*but* I am SOMEBODY!
People repeat.
LEADER: I may not know the current psychological jargon—*but*—I am SOMEBODY!
People repeat.
People stand up; each one faces one other person and holds hands.
LEADER: You may not be Mrs. Good Housekeeper—*but* you are SOMEBODY!
People repeat.
LEADER: You may not be Mr. Big Shot—*but* you are SOMEBODY!
People repeat.
LEADER: You may not have read the right books—*but*—you are SOMEBODY!
People repeat.
LEADER: You may not be able to balance your checkbook—*but*—you are SOMEBODY!
People repeat.
People sit down.
LEADER: Our children may be exasperating—*but*—they are SOMEBODY!
People repeat.
LEADER: Our children may spill things—*but* they are SOMEBODY!
People repeat.
LEADER: Our children may be stubborn—*but* they are SOMEBODY!
People repeat.
LEADER: Our children may wet their beds—*but* they are SOMEBODY!
People repeat.
All together hold hands (along rows if in pews).
LEADER: We may be frustrated—*but*—we are SOMEBODY!
People repeat.
LEADER: We may be supersensitive—*but*—we are SOMEBODY!
People repeat.
LEADER: We may be scared—*but*—we are SOMEBODY!
People repeat.

LEADER: We may be overconfident—*but*—we are SOMEBODY!
People repeat.
LEADER: In the beginning . . . God created . . . man.
People repeat.
LEADER: Male and female . . . He created . . . them.
People repeat.
LEADER: And God said . . . "Behold . . . They are good!"
People repeat.
LEADER: And God said . . . "They are . . . SOMEBODY!"
People repeat.
LEADER: And in the fullness of time. . . .
People repeat.
LEADER: God created us. . . .
People repeat.
LEADER: And he said. . . .
People repeat.
LEADER: "Behold! You are good."
People repeat.
LEADER: You are . . . SOMEBODY!
People repeat.
LEADER: I am SOMEBODY!
People repeat.
LEADER: You are SOMEBODY!
People repeat.
LEADER: Our children are SOMEBODY!
People repeat.
LEADER: We are SOMEBODY!
People repeat.
LEADER: Amen—Amen!
People repeat.

After using the litany, explain that the purpose of your school is to emphasize the "somebodyness" of each child enrolled. Go over the time schedule; emphasize its flexibility. Outline your goals and activities for the first few weeks and invite the parents' participation and suggestions, making it clear that their participation is not required but is heartily welcomed. Share your objectives for the use of interest centers.[9] You may do this in small groups with parents as leaders.

It is good to make a storage tote box (cubbie) for each group before school starts. These are corrugated paper boxes which are covered with contact paper and bound with tape (two inches wide). Clothesline rope handles are inserted in each end of the box, knotting them on the inside. These storage tote boxes are an invaluable aid. In each of these boxes are paper bags, size

[9] See pages 44-46.

0300, one for each child in the group. Each child's name is written on the upper left-hand corner of the paper bag, using manuscript lettering. The paper bags are filed alphabetically in each box, using first name starting letters as guides. As a child makes something to take home — such as paintings, collages, clay or wooden objects — they are put in his paper bag. Toys which have been brought from home are placed there, too. When the group goes to the playground, the tote box goes along. As parents call for the children, the teacher only needs to look in one spot for everything without having to paw through a whole assortment of other children's things to find what he or she is seeking. This is another way of affirming the value of each child.

Individual place mats for snacks can be made which will last the whole year. They are made out of the material which is used to package cold cuts of meat. This material comes in a large roll. Two pieces of the desired size, with colored tissue inserted between in various sizes and shapes, is bound with plumber's tape. These make beautiful place mats which really take the wear and tear. After snack time is over, the children take turns wiping them off with a damp sponge. The child's name again appears in the upper left-hand corner, and before long the child not only recognizes his place mat but also his name. Use a felt-tip marker of the permanent type so that the name will not wash off. Again, his place mat tells the child he belongs.

Each teacher should have the list of her children in chronological order, not for the purpose of categorizing the child but to insure that a card will be mailed to him in time for his special day, the day he was born. Cards, stamps, and a birthday button to wear on his special day at school all help parents to know that their child is being planned for at church. A gaily decorated hat is also made for the birthday child to wear during snack time. Sometimes at the last of the year the teachers make hats for everyone so that the summer birthday children can have theirs, too.

There should be an alphabetized master file of the names of the children as the school grows. One file should be made for Monday, Wednesday, Friday groups and one for Tuesday, Thursday groups. The cards are placed in the master file when the registration fee is received. To doublecheck this file, each day's receipts are recorded in a stenographer's notebook. Balancing receipts and cards daily eliminates many headaches and misunderstandings. Please note this is not a job for the teachers unless your school is very small. They really should have nothing to do with the bookkeeping mechanics. Many children will come in, however, with tuition checks pinned on them. The teacher will unpin them and place them in a special place where the person responsible for the bookkeeping can pick them up.

Attendance records are kept in each group so that teachers can keep a close check on absences and act out their concern if an absence seems prolonged and there has been no explanation for it. These charts should be made out before the opening of school. Careful planning helps the teacher to focus completely on the children instead of on details, and such attention says to the parent and the child that they are important and that you will take every precaution for their welfare.

❆❆ 9 ❆❆
What Are Our Objectives?
Centering Our Interests

We teach through relationships and with the use of interest centers. These centers are true to their name — centers of interest to the child. He has a free choice of them throughout the first hour of the morning's program. To help increase understanding of the essentiality of play in preschool education, the following objectives for each center have been developed:

A. *OBJECTIVES FOR THE USE OF THE MUSIC CENTER*
  1. For meeting the need of the preschool child for rhythmic movement and sound.
  2. For providing a natural outlet for feelings.
  3. For sharing — ideas, record player, and rhythm instruments.
  4. For freeing a tense child.
  5. For enjoying happy experiences — group or individual.
  6. For quiet — resting time.
  7. For simple accompaniment for teacher or pupil singing — or for finger painting.

B. *OBJECTIVES FOR THE ART CENTER*
  1. To give child satisfaction of creativity.
  2. To relieve tensions.
  3. To get rid of hostile feelings.
  4. To give opportunity for expression of good feelings (joy, happiness, sense of well-being).
  5. To allow child to achieve.
  6. To give child privacy in the group.
  7. To provide limits necessary for self-discipline.
  8. To give clues to the teacher through way child approaches material.
  9. To meet physical need for large muscle movement and manipulation.

C. *OBJECTIVES FOR BLOCKS*
  1. To give opportunity for problem solving.
  2. To give opportunity for sharing.
  3. To give opportunity for cooperative play.
  4. To make creative use of conflict in social situations with teacher guidance.

5. To give satisfaction through achievement.
6. To teach responsibility – picking up blocks and putting them on shelves in orderly way.
7. To give clues to teacher as to child's self-image.

D. *OBJECTIVES FOR THE BOOK CENTER*
   1. To enrich experiences of the session.
   2. To provide balance necessary in active morning.
   3. To stimulate thought and imagination.
   4. To accomplish Christian education objectives through story content – pictures and conversation.
   5. To provide fun.
   6. To emphasize session's purpose.
   7. To establish person-to-person relationship – teacher and child.
   8. To help shy or timid child.
   9. To encourage exploration and discovery of God's world.

E. *OBJECTIVES FOR HOME LIVING CENTER*
   1. To provide dramatic play – helps children recreate home experiences.
   2. To stimulate imagination.
   3. To equip them for father-mother (parental) roles.
   4. To help social adjustment.
   5. To develop cooperative spirit.
   6. To teach responsibility for orderliness.
   7. To teach respect for rights of others.
   8. To give child experience in identifying with others – a necessary Christian trait.
   9. To give opportunities to share.
   10. To provide outlet for good and bad emotions.
   11. To help child understand others through playing out the role.

F. *OBJECTIVES FOR WONDER TABLE*
   1. To associate mysteries with God.
   2. To bring about feelings of wonder and awe.
   3. To bring God close through opportunities for conversation with him and about him.
   4. To teach awareness of God's beauty and plan in the world.
   5. To give the child opportunity to share nature's treasures with others.
   6. To give opportunity to bring outdoors inside the room.

    7. To teach responsibility — watering plants, feeding pets, etc.

G. *OBJECTIVES FOR PICTURES*
1. To stimulate thought.
2. To arouse feelings of wonder.
3. To express appreciation and pleasure.
4. To emphasize morning's purpose.
5. To suggest activity.
6. To use only those recommended pictures of Jesus.
7. To encourage conversation and the sharing of ideas.
8. To limit indiscriminate use of pictures.

H. *OBJECTIVES FOR MISCELLANEOUS INTEREST CENTERS*
1. Grocery store in November
    a) To live out home experiences.
    b) To emphasize importance of others in providing our food.
        1) God's plan for food.
        2) Many helpers needed to provide it.
2. Doctor's office and/or hospital in January
    a) To act out feelings.
    b) To resolve negative feelings.
    c) To emphasize the importance of others in helping us keep well.
3. Filling station in January
    a) To create role of familiar helper.
    b) To stimulate imagination.
    c) To provide a plus for block and truck play.
4. Barber shop, beauty parlor, in February
    a) To emphasize maleness and femaleness.
    b) To provide opportunities for cooperative play.
    c) To help child understand others.

I. *PERCEPTUAL — MOTOR CENTER*
1. To give a good body image.
2. To give the feel of rhythm.
3. To help eye–hand coordination.
4. To give a sense of space.
5. To promote basic skills.
6. To help in communication.

⚛ 10 ⚛
What Tools Shall We Use?
Gathering Our Supplies

When are the rooms ready? What supplies should be on hand? What interest centers should be provided and how are they to be used? What makes a balanced morning's program? How often should the staff meet?

Your rooms are ready for your children when everything about them says invitingly to a child, "Come in, use me!" During the initial visit and experiencing of the room with his parents, the child has had many opportunities to feel his own worth through his contact with the teachers and the provisions they have made especially for him. He has felt, "This is a good place to be!"

Most denominational church school teachers' guides list many of the basic supplies which should be on hand. However, at the risk of being possibly redundant, and because too often one finds, in examining budgets, a lack of awareness of the importance of these items, they are listed. Many of these supplies have to be replenished regularly and should be purchased from the monthly budget for such purposes. Others are permanent and seldom need replacement. For the sake of facility these supplies are being listed as adjuncts to the interest areas where they are to be used most frequently.

ART CENTER
Double easel, with legs cut off—Commercial school easels are all too high.
Paint brushes—8 per room—Artista #111, 1 inch wide.
White newsprint—18″ x 24″.
Powdered tempera in 4 basic colors. Add brown and orange in fall, black and white in winter, pastel colors in spring. Never leave more than 4 colors on one side of easel.
Tide or Ivory Snow—Can be secured in quantities from laundromats. For mixing powdered paint: Use half and half, add water enough to facilitate paint flow and yet avoid too many drips.
Newspapers—For covering easel, lining trays, and for floor protection.
Felt-tip pen—For putting child's name in upper left-hand corner, using manuscript writing.
Sponges for cleanup.
Styrofoam coffee cups for paint. (These may be salvaged from coffee hours.) Paint can be mixed in these and placed in trays. They can be thrown away, eliminating a disagreeable cleanup task.

Drying rack—For paintings. Available from Creative Playthings, Princeton, N.J.

Pinch clothespins—For hanging up paintings, for covering easel with newspaper, for securing newsprint, for sponge painting, for string painting, and for fastening pairs of boots together.

Cold clay materials—Made from flour, salt, and vegetable oil. Children may mix ingredients with supervision.
4 c. flour, 1 c. salt, $1\frac{1}{4}$ c. water, $\frac{1}{4}$ c. oil. Add powdered tempera to dry materials for color.

10 pound package wet clay—See your local art supply store or a ceramist. They will be able to tell you where clay is available in your area.

4 trays—such as used in cafeterias.

Commercially prepared fingerpaint—Prang's Media Mix, to which powdered paint is added.

Pastels or brilliant colored chalk.

Powdered milk—for buttermilk painting.

Bits of sponge.

Spools, pegs, and blocks for printing.

Mr. Sketch colored felt watercolor markers.

Crayons—Prang Crayonnex Stubbies 253x—16

Scissors—blunt. Try to secure with holes large enough to accommodate two fingers. Have two pairs of left-handed scissors. Tie red string on to identify.

Newsprint—12″ x 18″.

Poster paper in assorted colors, 12″ x 18″.

Duotone paper in assorted colors, 12″ x 18″.

Economy Manila—12″ x 18″.

Coated paper—12″ x 18″.

Tissue paper pomps—available from Crystal Tissue, Middletown, Ohio.

Rubber cement—be sure to open windows when using.

Paint thinner for cleaning brushes—keep out of the reach of children.

Small jars with screw caps for cement.

Paste brushes with 6-inch handles.

Collage materials.

Items for gadget printing—plastic forks and kitchen items, such as potato masher.

Stapler and staples and cardboard pieces.

Masking tape.

Straws, tongue depressors, cotton swabs, popsicle sticks, bits of yarn, ribbon, toothpicks.

Brayers (printer's hand inking rollers).

Hardware cloth and corrugated boards for rubbings.

Coated wires from telephone cables.

BLOCK CENTER

Block cart—available from Community Playthings, Rifton, N.Y.

Unit blocks.

Large hollow blocks.

Large trucks, boats, airplanes, derricks.

Trains and small sizes of above.

Wooden animals and farm workers.

Assortment of hats—fireman, policeman, construction worker.

Prop boxes, tool kits, clocks, wires, wheels.

BOOK CENTER

Book rack, preferably on casters.

Books to be found under monthly resources and also under Personal Identity Book list.

Pictures to stimulate conversation and not to be used as wall decor.

Puzzles—See Judy, Sifo, or Playskool catalogs.

Wooden puzzle rack.

Table toys—such as riga-jigs, pegboards, felt boards, form boards, plastic shapes, small toy animals, cars, and small muscle manipulative toys.

Audiovisual equipment—viewers, slides, tape recorder, projector, films and filmstrips listed under monthly resources.

PERMANENT PRINT SUGGESTIONS FOR WALLS OF BOOK CENTER

Boy with Book, James Chapin, Oestreicher Catalog, 93 West 46th Street, New York, New York.

Carpenter Shop, Reed Champion, United Church Press, 1505 Race St., Philadelphia, Pennsylvania.

Child with Dove, Picasso, Oestreicher Catalog.

Christ with Children, Bella Vichon, Axtert Prints, Westport, Connecticut.

He Prayeth Best, Margaret Tarrant, Oestreicher Catalog.

Jesus and Children, James Seward, Nursery Packet, American Baptist Board of Education and Publication, Valley Forge, Pennsylvania.

Mother and Child, Kathe Kollwitz.

The Picture Book, James Chapin, Oestreicher Catalog.

HOMEMAKING CENTER

Kitchen unit—Sink, refrigerator, cupboard, and stove. Small table and two chairs, broom and dustpan, dry mop, high chair, tablecloth, dishes, pans, nursing bottle, baby's divided dish, empty food cartons, uncolored dough, cookie cutters, rolling pin, oven pans, lunch pail, picnic basket, telephone.

Bedroom unit—Bed, bedding, dresser, full-length mirror, and coat rack, dress-up clothes, including men's hats, shoes, wallets, ties, razors without blades, attaché case, women's clothing, including girdles, dresses, shoes, hats, purses, jewelry, doctor and nurse's smocks, stethoscope, disposable syringe without needle, empty toilet article containers.

MUSIC CENTER

Record player.

Autoharp or guitar.

Tone bells.

Rhythm instruments, including good drum, castanets, jingle clogs, wrist and ankle bells, sand blocks, rhythm sticks, hand drums, tambourines, tone blocks, triangles, cymbals, and maracas.

Good selection of recordings, including rest music, rhythm records, Mr. Rogers records (available from Judson Book Stores), and "Ramo" (available from Creative Materials Library, 709—17 Ave. S., Nashville, Tenn.).

PLAYGROUND

Sandbox with shovels, scoops, pails, muffin tins.

Climbing apparatus—Fireman's gym, commando gym, tree logs, ladders, knotted rope.

Wheeled toys—wagons and tricycles—for paved area.

Rocking seesaws.

Slide.

Small trampoline.

Foxhole barrels.

Large industrial spools.

Waterplay materials to be used inside and out: plastic wading pool, wooden blocks, containers for pouring, tubing, 3" brushes for water painting, and pails.

Hose, pipe fittings, old faucet or pump, fish poles, big boxes, and containers.

PERCEPTUAL MOTOR CENTER

Feely bags, made by placing different objects in a plain brown bag or box with holes in it. The children then identify the objects by their "feel."

Blackboard.

Walking beams.

Balance board.

Ladders, to be used outside.

Waterplay materials as listed above.

Obstacle course materials.

Ropes, balls, bean bags.

Tumbling mat.

WONDER CENTER

Aquarium—fish, snails, tadpoles.

Terrarium—growing plants.

Live animals, such as guinea pigs and gerbils.

Large magnifying glass.

Prism.

Nature materials, shells, seed pods, stones.

Cocoon—available from General Biological Supply House, 8300 S. Hoyne, Chicago, Illinois.

Magnets, iron filings.

WOODWORKING CENTER

Workbench with vise.

Tools—saws, hammers, hand drill.

Soft pine scraps, nails, screws, bottle caps.

MISCELLANEOUS MATERIALS

Resting mats—made of plastic. Available from Sterling Products, Minneapolis, Minn.

Kleenex, Band-Aids.
Bowls for mixing clay.
Baskets for snacks. Pitchers for juice.
Paper cups.

It is a good idea to post at teacher eye level the objectives for the use of each interest center in order to insure that they are being used properly. Too often there is a temptation to structure the use of these centers in such a way that all creativity is lost and the child is told how to use them. We have to be on guard constantly against manipulating or using children in ways which might be *bad news* to them.

A balanced morning's program takes into account the need of each child to feel secure, the need for activity, the need for quiet, the need for creativity, and the need for food and elimination. Most nursery schools find that a two-and-a-half-hour morning or afternoon for four-year-olds provides for an hour's free choice of interest centers; forty-five minutes for the routines of toileting, snack, and rest; a total group experience of fifteen minutes; and thirty minutes of outdoor play.

Most three-year-olds are not ready for a total group experience until late in the year. However, they do group themselves often in small groups of two or three to hear a story, look at books or pictures, do body plays and rhythm, or sing with the autoharp.

Teachers should be on the job one-half hour before school starts and as long after dismissal as is needed to restore the room to order. This may mean some janitorial work. No child should ever walk into a disorderly room when he arrives for his day in the church. On the other side of the coin, each child should assume the responsibility for picking up after himself.

Staff meetings should be held every two weeks for the purpose of evaluation, planning, and study. Every teacher should be very familiar with the *Resource Portfolio of Nursery Education Handbook* (American Baptist Board of Education and Publication). Other good books for study include the following:

Anderson, Phoebe M., *Religious Living with Nursery Children*. Philadelphia: United Church Press, 1956.
Cohen, Dorothy H., and Stern, V., *Children*. New York: Teachers College Press, Columbia University, 1958.
Hemphill, Martha Locke, *Partners in Teaching Young Children*. Valley Forge: Judson Press, 1972.
Hollander, H. Cornelia, *Portable Workshop for Pre-School Teachers*. Garden City, N.Y.: Doubleday & Company, Inc.

Howe, Reuel L., *Herein Is Love*. Valley Forge: Judson Press, 1961.

Hymes, Jesild, *The Child Under Six*. Englewood Cliffs, N.J.: Prentice-Hall, Inc., 1963.

Jersild, Arthur T., *When Teachers Face Themselves*. New York: Teachers College Press, Columbia University, 1955.

Missildine, W. Hugh, *Your Inner Child of the Past*. New York: Simon and Schuster, Inc., 1963.

Powell, John, *Why Am I Afraid to Tell You Who I Am?* Chicago: Argus Communications.

Read, Katherine H., *The Nursery School*. Philadelphia: W. B. Saunders Company, 1966.

Reeves, Katherine, *Children's Ways and Wants*. Darien, Conn.: Educational Publishers, Inc.

Schulz, Florence B., *Summer with Nursery School Children*. Philadelphia: United Church Press, 1958.

❧❧ II ❧❧
The Time Is Now
Beginning the School Year

There are two programs which are fairly new and most significant for self-actualization which your church can offer to your children. One of these is a motor-exploratory program, and the other is a language-arts program which helps a child identify feelings and verbalize them.

A program of motor exploration in a nursery school is designed for just this function — to challenge children to explore various ways of moving. Helping children to feel and to know where they are and to know what their bodies are doing is fundamental to helping them feel successful. Most of the activities in a program for the young child are designed to help children know what their bodies are doing; the rest are to help with the problem of balance.

A fifteen-minute group time with four-year-olds, once a week, is a good basis for programming with two main approaches. One approach is to use an obstacle course which gives the children the opportunity to crawl under, climb over, squeeze between, jump off, slide along, jump over, jump onto, roll over, and squirm. Chairs, two-by-fours, large blocks, tables, ladders, and many other available objects can be used to set up an obstacle course. Rope stretched from one table leg to another, for instance, can be used to increase the challenge.

The greatest problem comes with monitoring the course. It needs to be so planned that children are not bunched or bottled up behind one task which may demand more time than another. Starting children at different points in the course helps avoid this problem. It is most important to watch the course closely to see that the children do the tasks individually, and thus have a chance to see and feel what is happening. If they bunch up, pushing each other, following one another too closely on the equipment, little learning takes place.

A child trying to walk on a two-by-four laid on the floor needs to look straight ahead, focusing on a target, and to walk slowly. For only by controlling his eyes and actually coming to balance does he learn. Going fast across a board gets him across but teaches him nothing.

Rolling, as a learning experience, needs to be done with the child lying flat, in a straight line. Rolling, as many do when uninstructed, with head up and weight on elbows, does nothing to help a child learn about his vertical axis.

A ladder laid flat on the ground, and later raised on small blocks, presents a good challenge. Walking up or down a slanted board, frontwards, backwards, and sidewards is fun. In all activities, controlled slow movements are desirable. It is worth noting that the children who function efficiently use their eyes to control their body movements. Many inefficient children have not learned to use their eyes to control their movements. Speed too often covers a lack of skill.

The more structured type of programs, suggested later in this book under the heading "Motor Exploration," can be done with or without musical accompaniment. A piano, if an accompanist is available, adds to the fun and feeling of rhythm and working with music. Rhythm instruments, such as tom-toms, work well as timekeepers, and many activities can be done to a chanting beat. A record player lacks the flexibility and sensitivity to a group that only a person can give.

The group programs which are developed on a monthly basis start with simple activities. Each activity is done only once with a particular group, being repeated only when the group has failed to grasp the idea or if it is being learned anew. Many are so simple that the children can follow the instructions satisfactorily at once.

The program is planned so that individual activities follow each other closely and easily, from standing to sitting, with quiet activities after active exercises. The children are grouped informally. A circle may be formed at the beginning, and after that the children stay where they happen to be, following the last activity.

Watch the children! Many times their attempts or suggestions or "Watch Me!" are something you will want to use either right then or later on. They will be showing you how to *teach* them.

The personal identification in the language arts program is built around the use of pictures which portray feelings and moods and the conversation which these motivate. Children identify with these feelings, verbalize them, and to some degree both understand and accept their feelings. In the field for three- and four-year-olds, there have been many new books coming from the Menninger Clinic, the Institute of Mental Health, curriculum materials from various denominations, and from sensitive writers who feel with children.

Some good titles follow:

Books from Behavioral Publications
Fassler, Joan, *All Alone with Daddy*. New York: Behavioral Publications, Inc., 1969.
_____, *The Man of the House*. New York: Behavioral Publications, Inc., 1969.
_____, *One Little Girl*. New York: Behavioral Publications, Inc., 1969.
De Regniers, Beatrice S., and Hogrogian, N., *The Day Everybody Cried*. New York: The Viking Press, Inc., 1967.
Holland, Ruth, *A Bad Day*. New York: David McKay Co., Inc., 1964.
Lobel, Arnold, *Prince Bertram the Bad*. New York: Harper & Row, Publishers, 1963.

Menninger Clinic Books
Watson, Jane W., *Look at Me Now*. Racine, Wis.: Western Publishing Company, Inc., 1971.
_____, *My Friend the Babysitter*. Racine, Wis.: Western Publishing Company, Inc., 1971.
_____, *Sometimes I Get Angry*. Racine, Wis.: Western Publishing Company, Inc., 1971.
_____, *Sometimes I'm Afraid*. Racine, Wis.: Western Publishing Company, Inc., 1971.
Viorst, Judith, *I'll Fix Anthony*. New York: Harper & Row, Publishers, 1969.

It helps with the routine of the first days if the children arrive wearing the name tags which they have picked up at the Open House the week before. Name tags should be made out of oak tag as this is more durable and the child will probably need to wear it during the entire first week. A length of rug yarn, purchasable at variety stores, makes a good necklace for the name tag. Teachers also should wear the same kind of name tag, and a large replica of the name tag can be mounted outside the classroom door, using a loop of masking tape to hold it, to further identify the child with the room. A list of the children's names in the group also should be posted outside the door. Anything which helps the child and his mother to feel that he is expected and that he belongs will help them both.

A gummed name tag should be made out ahead of time for each child. This tag should be affixed to the back of each child when he goes out to the playground.

What are some of the feelings which these children may be having as they start nursery school? What should the emphasis be during these first few weeks? What purposes should they achieve? What resources can we use? What activities can we plan?

Many of our children will be coming in with the unverbalized question, "Am I big enough?" They are confused; for at one time they may hear that they are too big to be doing something which they have done, while at the next moment they hear that they are too little. When one minute a child hears, "Don't act like a baby!" and the next minute he is told, "You are just a baby," he wonders whether he is little or big.

Some children will have anxieties about leaving their mothers; others will have anxiety about their adequacy; and still others are not too happy about leaving a younger sibling at home to enjoy the full monopoly of his mother.

The emphasis for the first month of school will be on growing. In every way we will affirm the child. When something is hard, we will be sure to help the child feel that some things are hard for each one of us, thus building his faith in himself that he *can*. To be sure, we need to see that he experiences successes; yet, on the other hand, we will do nothing for him which he can do for himself.

Watchwords for the teacher are "take it easy." Show the child in every way that he is big enough, that you are in his corner, and that the church is a very good place to be.

If there is any difficulty on either the parent's part or the child's at the separation, encourage the mother to stay until they both feel more comfortable about it. Be very sure to take this up at the parents' orientation meeting so that the parent understands about this policy ahead of time. Sometimes one may hear a child being scolded for crying or even threatened with punishment if he does cry. Any positive feelings he may have about his adequacy suffer because of this.

Books which may be used during the month of September with individuals, small groups, or total groups are listed below. The "personal identity" books, so-called because the child identifies personally with the story and builds a positive image of himself as he responds to it, are starred throughout.

BOOKS

★ Beim, Jerrold, *The Smallest Boy in the Class*. New York: William Morrow & Co., Inc., 1949.

Bryant, Bernice, *Let's Be Friends*. Chicago: Childrens Press.

Cassidy, Clara, *We Like Kindergarten.* New York: Golden Press, Inc., 1965.

★ Cohen, M., *Will I Have a Friend?* New York: The Macmillan Company, 1967.

Fritz, Jean, *Growing Up.* Chicago: Rand McNally & Co.

Green, M. M., *Is It Hard? Is It Easy?* New York: William R. Scott, Inc., 1960.

Hitte, Kathryn, *Lost and Found.* Nashville: Abingdon Press, 1951.

House, Wanda Rogers, *Peter Goes to School.* New York: Wonder Books, Inc.

Jackson, Kathryn and Byron, *Jerry at School.* New York: Golden Books, Inc., 1965.

Kaufman, Joe, *Big and Little.* New York: Golden Press, Inc., 1966.

★ Keats, Ezra J., *Whistle for Willie.* New York: The Viking Press, Inc., 1964.

Krasilovsky, Phyllis, *The Very Little Boy.* Garden City, N.Y.: Doubleday & Company, Inc., 1953.

_____, *The Very Little Girl.* Garden City, N.Y.: Doubleday & Company, Inc., 1953.

Kraus, Robert, *The Littlest Rabbit.* New York: Harper & Row, Publishers, 1961.

★ Krauss, Ruth, *The Growing Story.* New York: Harper & Row, Publishers, 1947.

Podendorf, Illa, *True Book of Animal Babies.* Chicago: Childrens Press, 1955.

★ Rice, Elizabeth, *I'm Alvin.* Austin, Texas: Steck-Vaughn Company, 1967.

Schlein, Miriam, *Big Lion, Little Lion.* Chicago: Albert Whiteman & Co., 1964.

_____, *Billy the Littlest One.* Chicago: Albert Whitman & Co., 1966.

Schwartz, Elizabeth and Charles, *When Animals Are Babies.* New York: Holiday House, Inc., 1964.

Selsam, Millicent, *All Kinds of Babies.* New York: Scholastic Book Services, 1971.

_____, *When an Animal Grows.* New York: Harper & Row, Publishers, 1966.

Steiner, Charlotte, *I'd Rather Stay with You.* New York: The Seabury Press, Inc., 1965.

Zolotov, Charlotte, *I Want to Be Little.* New York: Abelard-Schuman Limited, 1966.

FILMSTRIPS AND MOVIES

Filmstrips which may be used with small or total groupings during the month of September:

Animal Babies, Childrens Press, Chicago, Illinois.

Big Brothers Are Fun, Family Filmstrips, Hollywood, California.

Growing Up, Jam Handy, Detroit, Michigan.

The House Next Door, Family Filmstrips, Hollywood, California.

Joy of Being You, Division of Scholastic Magazine, Inc., New York, New York.

The Loose Tooth, Jam Handy, Detroit, Michigan.

The New Baby, Jam Handy, Detroit, Michigan.
Something New, Family Filmstrips, Hollywood, California.
We Grow, Jam Handy, Detroit, Michigan.

Fun movies which might be scheduled during the first month of school for children are: *Sebastian the Scatter Brain,* available from Contemporary Films, McGraw-Hill, 828 Custer, Evanston, IL 60202, and *If I Were An Animal,* available from Three Prong, 267 West 25th St., New York, NY 10001. It might be well, at the first meeting of the teachers, for them to view and discuss a film like *Chromophobia,* available from Mass Media Ministries, 2116 N. Charles St., Baltimore, Maryland. It points out the effects of uniformity.

GAME

Game for the four- and five-year-olds:
"Where Is Susie?" from *Come Sing with Me,* Margaret Crain McNeil (Judson Press, 1972). Sing to "Frere Jacque" tune. Repeat each line.

> Where is Susie? *Repeat*
> Here I am! *Repeat*
> We are glad to see you. *Repeat*
> You're our friend! *Repeat*

MOTOR EXPLORATION

Work on body image, one's own space, and relaxing concepts. Play statue.
Run on tiptoe and stop on command.
Learn space words. Chant using a beat:

> Hands to the front *and*
> Hands to the back *and*
> Hands way up high *and*
> Hands way down low *and*
> Hands on the ground *and*
> Hands on your ears *and*
> Hands on your nose *and*
> Hands on your eyes!

(Vary by doing this whole exercise with eyes shut.)

Pretend floor is sticky and walk around.

How many ways can you move your head? Touch the floor with your head.

Obstacle course:
Step over 12 inch high board.
Go under a board raised two feet high.
Walk forward on a two-by-four on the floor.
Sit on balance board.
Listen to sound with eyes closed and point in direction from whence
it came.

Use Raggedy Ann concept for relaxation:
Raggedy Ann was so tired her head went flop, flop.
Raggedy Ann was so tired her arms went flop, flop.
Raggedy Ann was so tired her knees went flop, flop.
Raggedy Ann was so tired she went flop, flop,
All the way down!

Conversation which may be used to establish structure:
"Once you were so little you could not talk. Every one of you was once
a baby. You could not walk. But, every day you grew! You grew big
enough to sit up. You grew big enough to walk. You grew big enough to
come to nursery school. You are still growing and you are big enough
when you learn this song, "Put the Toys Away" (in *Come Sing with Me*,
Margaret Crain McNeil [Judson Press, 1972]), to help put the toys away.
When you hear "Please Come Here" (same source), you sit on the floor
in front of the teacher or, if she is at the door, you go and stand with
her."

Conversation geared to establish a feeling of specialness. "Your
birthday is special. Your name is special. Everyone of us is special." As you write names on paintings, speak of it as having
a special meaning.

BODY PLAYS
"Sometimes I'm Very Tall"
Sometimes I'm very tall *(children stand and reach high)*
Sometimes I'm very small *(crouch on floor)*
Sometimes tall *(stand high)*
Sometimes small *(crouch)*
Now I'm just myself *(back in sitting position)*

Sing to the tune "Oats, Peas, Beans":
I saw a building big and high *(arms high)*
It seemed to reach up to the sky
A great big door opened wide *(arms out)*
For boys and girls to come inside.

"Hands to Help With," *Nursery Songs for Fall and Winter*
(Nashville, Tenn.: United Methodist Church).

Mr. Jack-in-the-Box

Marion B. Duke

M.B.D.

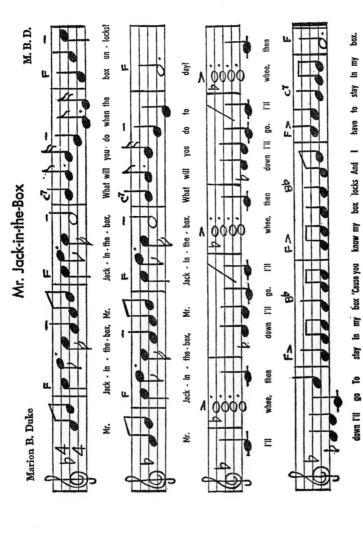

The children are locked in their "boxes" until they pop up three times on "Whee!" Such fun!

SONGS
Transition Song
Sing to the tune "Farmer in the Dell":

> We're putting——away
> We're putting——away
> We'll make our room
> All neat and clean
> We're putting——away.

Songs from *Come Sing with Me,* Margaret Crain McNeil (Valley Forge: Judson Press, 1972).
"Child of God"
"Glad to Be Me"
"Big Enough"
"You Are Special"
"A New Friend"

GRACE
Sing to the tune "Frere Jacque":

> God, we thank you.
> God, we thank you,
> For this day,
> For this day,
> And for all our good friends,
> And for all our good times,
> Thank you, God.

RECORDINGS
Records which may be used from Children's Record Guild, 100 Sixth Ave., New York, New York:
"A Visit to My Friend"
"Nothing to Do"

ACTIVITIES
Spool printing: Each child decorates his own paper bag cubbie. Mix up powdered paint in foil pan, adding detergent and water. Fold a Kleenex, place in the paint to absorb it, and use as ink pad for the spool. Have two or three colors and several spools in each pan.
Easel painting.
Cold clay.
Sponge painting.
Paper tearing: Use poster paper. After paper is torn, let child make a collage of the bits.
Decorate adding machine tape: Measure height of child. Show him how much he has grown since he was a baby. Measure off twenty-one inches, and tear off adding-machine tape to illustrate. Let child decorate with watercolor felt markers.

Sing to tune "Farmer in the Dell":

> You are bigger than you were.
> You are bigger than you were.
> Heigh, ho, the Derry-O,
> You are bigger than you were.

"I'm Special" stickers: Use after seeing the filmstrip *Joy of Being You.* Use gummed name tags. Put child's thumb on ink pad and let him print it on the gummed tag. Write "I'm Special" and let him wear it home.

Finger painting: Use trays and newsprint for monoprinting.

Bootie and foot tracing: Three-year-olds do not use scissors. Cut out bootie shapes in pink and blue colors for all who cannot handle scissors. Let child paste onto manila paper. Place on floor and let him put his foot over the bootie. Trace around it with a felt-tip pen, and he can see how much his foot has grown.

Fall Is Here!
Planning for October

You have had three or four weeks, or more accurately nine to twelve sessions, with your four-year-olds and six to eight sessions with your three-year-olds. You are beginning to know each child. As you seek to empathize with each one, you are becoming aware of needs which he may have and also his interests. A morning's program is only as good as its relevancy to these needs, interests, and the status quo. Someone has spoken of this as the indigenous curriculum. A part of this here-and-nowness, it would seem, should be to build a few sessions around Halloween. Though many Protestant churches do not observe All Saint's Day, Halloween is very much a part of every young child's life. National candy manufacturers prepare special packages for the "Trick or Treat" set and Madison Avenue does the rest. One nursery school child made the remark that Halloween was "much more funner" than Thanksgiving.

Three-year-olds are often frightened by masks, and it might be well to have a few simple masks in the dress-up box for a couple of weeks before Halloween. They can experience that feeling of fear and play with it in the security of the nursery school room.

BOOKS

Books which may be used during the month:

Bancroft, Henrietta, *Down Come the Leaves.* New York: Thomas Y. Crowell Company, 1961.

Buckley, Helen, *Where Did Josie Go?* New York: Lothrop, Lee & Shepard Co., Inc., 1962.

Dow, Katherine, *My Time of Year.* New York: Henry Z. Walck, Inc., 1961.

Ets, Marie Hall, *Play with Me.* New York: The Viking Press, Inc., 1955.

Foster, Doris V., *A Pocketful of Seasons.* New York: Lothrop, Lee & Shepard Co., Inc.

★Haas, Dorothy, *A Special Place for Johnny.* Philadelphia: Whitman Publishing Co.

Howell, Ruth R., *Everything Changes.* New York: Atheneum Publishers, 1968.

Kessler, Ethel and Leonard, *The Big Red Bus.* Garden City, N.Y.: Doubleday & Company, Inc., 1964.

Miles, Betty, *A Day of Autumn.* New York: Alfred A. Knopf, Inc., 1967.

Miller, Edna, *Mousekin's Golden House*. Englewood Cliffs, N.J.: Prentice-Hall, Inc., 1964.

Moore, Lilian, *Once Upon a Season*. Nashville: Abingdon Press, 1962.

Nielson, Jean, *Green Eyes*. New York: Funk & Wagnalls, 1955.

Parker, Bertha M., *Fall Is Here*. New York: Golden Press, Inc., 1958.

Pohl, Louis, *It's Really Nice*. Boston: Little, Brown and Company, 1960.

Roorback, Harriet A., *I Learn About Sharing*. Nashville: Abingdon Press.

Slobodkina, Esphyr, *Caps for Sale*. New York: William R. Scott, Inc., 1947.

Tresselt, Alvin, *Johnny Maple-Leaf*. New York: Lothrop, Lee & Shepard Co., Inc., 1951.

Wilde, Irma, *Dress Up Parade*. New York: Wonder Books, Inc.

Wolcott, Carolyn Muller, *God Gave Us Seasons*. Nashville: Abingdon Press, 1958.

FILMSTRIPS AND MOVIES

Filmstrips which may be used:

God's Autumn World, Family Filmstrips, Hollywood, California
God Cares Through a Dependable World, Family Filmstrips
The Jolly Bus, Family Filmstrips
Molly's Blocks, Family Filmstrips
Molly's Dollies, Family Filmstrips
Mrs. Squirrel's Family, Society Visual Education, Diversey Pkwy., Chicago, Illinois
Ping, Weston Woods, Weston, Connecticut

Movies which may be rented from Encyclopedia Britannica and Three Prong Studios:

Animals in Autumn, Encyclopedia Britannica, 425 N. Michigan Ave., Chicago, IL 60611
Children in Autumn, Encyclopedia Britannica
Where Does My Street Go? Three Prong Studios, 267 West 25th St., New York, NY 10001

MOTOR EXPLORATION

Continue work on "own space." Pretend to paint it with wide brush sweeps to the front, side, back, and other side.

Practice dodging skills.

Lie on the floor relaxed. Stretch tight as a string and as thin. Let go.

Wrap each thumb with coated wire piece. Draw a pumpkin on the floor with each of your thumbs. Put in eyes, nose, and mouth using only the thumb.

Imitate Halloween characters: witches galloping, spacemen walking, tigers on all fours, ghosts flopping.

Continue head exercises, pointing to ears, eyes, nose, chin, defining how much of the body is the head.

BODY PLAYS (Sources unknown. Traditional.) :

I'm an old maple tree,	*(Stand with*
And I have so many leaves.	*outstretched*
What shall I do with them?	*arms.)*
If you please!	
Wait a little while	*(Whirl with*
Till the fall winds blow.	*WHOOSH and*
OH! OH! WHOOSH! Down they go!	*fall down.)*
A little squirrel	*(Use left arm for*
with a bushy tail	*tree making a hole*
Goes frisking all	*by putting finger*
around!	*tips to thumb. Right*
And every day	*hand scurries on the*
He stores away	*floor, climbs up*
The nuts	*left arm and sticks*
That he has found.	*nuts in the hole.)*
A pumpkin round	*(Make circle with arms.)*
and very fat,	*(Hands together, high*
A tiny witch	*over head.*
with a pointy hat,	*Circle eyes with*
The scary eyes	*fingers.)*
of a big black cat—	
That makes Halloween.	

SONGS

"Gray Squirrel," *Our Song* (C. C. Birchard & Company, 1952).

"Who's Behind That False Face?" *Music for Young Americans* (American Book Co.)

Sing to the tune, "Farmer in the Dell":

> The owl goes Hoo!
> The owl goes Hoo!
> Heigh Ho on Halloween
> The owl goes Hoo!
>
> The ghost goes Boo!
> The ghost goes Boo!
> Heigh Ho on Halloween
> The ghost goes Boo!

GRACE: "Johnny Appleseed Song."

ACTIVITIES

Activities which may be used:

Handprint trees: Use large sheet of newsprint. Have children place hand in pan of any one of red, yellow, green, brown, or orange paint, and then print on the newsprint.

Treasure hunt: Have children decorate no. 8 paper sack to take home for a fall treasure trip with family.

3-D mural: Make of treasures from paper bag.

Fall mobile: Balance a branch on thread, and tie on some of the interesting treasures.

Leaf rubbings: Place leaf, vein side up, under tracing paper. Rub with side of crayon.

Leaf transparencies: Take a walk and hunt for pretty leaves. Put each one in waxed-paper sandwich bag in which a few crayon shavings have been sprinkled. Press with low heated iron on pad of newspapers.

Leaf people: Mount leaf on economy manila. Add arms, legs, and head.

Crumpled tissue fall trees: Crumple 2" x 2" squares of fall-colored tissue and mount on manila paper. Crayon trunk.

Sponge-paint fall trees.

Field trips: To a farm or large garden to see pumpkins growing and to pick some. To apple orchards to pick apples. To tractor salesrooms.

Carve pumpkin.

Paper-bag masks: Use no. 16 sacks. Cut out holes for eyes ahead of time and cut away top half of paper bag. Let children decorate masks with felt-tip markers. Save top half of paper bag for making Indian headbands next month.

Seed collages: Use pumpkin seeds and Indian corn which children have shelled. Corn cobs sliced make an interesting effect on a collage. Save some pumpkin seeds to plant in the spring and others to roast next month.

ꙮ 13 ꙮ
A Time of Thanksgiving
Planning for November

After Halloween there is the letdown which comes after any celebration, particularly if you have allowed the children to dress up and have a parade and parties. Therefore, this is a good time to add a new interest center. The children with a minimum of props can make a supermarket out of blocks, tables, and boards. Teachers should have large paper bags on hand, also empty cartons, cans, and boxes. Every day the children will add to the store. Shirt smocks, doll-buggy grocery carts, cash registers — all add to the play. Many props, such as large food posters, can be secured from local markets.

The emphases for the month are all built around food — how it grows, people who help us get food, the wonder of it all, and practice in the formation of prayers of Thanksgiving.

BOOKS

Bannister, C., *A Child's Grace*. New York: E. P. Dutton & Co., Inc., 1938.

Curry, Nancy, *An Apple Is Red*. Glendale, Calif.: Bowmar Publishing Corp.

Dillard, Polly, *My Thank-You Book*. Nashville: Broadman Press, 1964.

Goodspeed, J. M., *Let's Go to the Supermarket*. New York: G. P. Putnam's Sons, 1958.

Green, Mary M., *Everybody Eats*. New York: William R. Scott, Inc., 1961.

Greene, Carla, *I Want to Be a Storekeeper*. Chicago: Childrens Press.

Hoban, Russell, *Bread and Jam for Frances*. New York: Harper & Row, Publishers, 1964.

★Hunter, Elizabeth M., *Robespierre*. Philadelphia: United Church Press.

Krauss, Ruth, *The Carrot Seed*. New York: Harper & Row, Publishers, 1945.

Lenski, Lois, *I Went for a Walk*. New York: Henry Z. Walck, Inc., 1958.

Martin, Bill and Bernard, *The Brave Little Indian*. New York: Holt, Rinehart & Winston, Inc.

Martin, Dick, *The Apple Book*. New York: Golden Press, Inc.

McCaw, Mabel N., *Orange Juice for Terry*. Nashville: Broadman Press, 1962.

★Meek, Pauline P., *The Broken Vase*. Richmond, Va.: John Knox Press, 1965.

Scheer, Julian, *Rain Makes Applesauce*. New York: Holiday House, Inc., 1964.

Vogel, Ilse-Margret, *Hello Henry*. New York: Parents' Magazine Press, 1965.

White, Mary S., *I Know Why We Give Thanks*. Nashville: Broadman Press, 1956.

FILMSTRIPS AND MOVIES

Filmstrips which may be used during the month:

Donald's Apple Orchard, Society Visual Education, Chicago, Illinois
Fussbunny, Society Visual Education
Gathering Eggs, Jam Handy, Detroit, Michigan
God Cares Through Growing Things, Family Filmstrips, Hollywood, California
God's Care in Winter, Family Filmstrips
The Grocer, Jam Handy
How Apples Grow, Society Visual Education
Milking, Jam Handy
Shopping at the Supermarket, Jam Handy
Shopping with Mother, Family Filmstrips
Thanksgiving with Carol and Peter, Society Visual Education

Movie:

Uncle Jim's Dairy Farm. Free film from Association Films, 561 Hillgrove Ave., La Grange, IL 60525.

MOTOR EXPLORATION

Gallop, changing the starting foot often.
Walk backwards, looking straight ahead; then tiptoe backwards; then jump backwards.
Work on tongue movements and also shoulders.
Shoulder movements include putting hands on opposite shoulder, swing arm to feel movement. Move each shoulder up, down, front, backward. Touch shoulder to floor, to knee.
Use rhythm sticks — tap to music in front, to side, to back. Change hands in back and tap to other side.
Touch stick to shoulder and other end to floor. Put stick to knee and shoulder in same manner.

BODY PLAYS (Sources unknown):

Way up high in an apple tree,
(Raise arms above head, index fingers making two apples)
Two little apples smiled at me.
I shook that tree as hard as I could,
  (Shake arms)
And down came the apples.
  (Drop one hand and then the other)
MMM—were they good!

Mr. Turkey's tail is big and wide.
(Spread both hands)
He swings it when he walks.
(Swing hands from side to side)
His neck is long, his chin is red.
He gobbles when he talks.
(Hands together under chin, open up and down)

SONGS

Songs from *Come Sing with Me,* Margaret Crain McNeil (Judson Press, 1972).

Thank you songs:
"Thank you, God"
"Rejoice, Give Thanks and Sing"
"We Give Thanks"
"Give Thanks to the Lord"
"Now Thank We All Our God"

Other songs to be used this month:
"Good News! Thanksgiving's Coming"
"Pumpkin Song"

ACTIVITIES

Field trips might include trips to a bakery, dairy farm, dairy plant, turkey farm, or back room of the supermarket.

Make applesauce: The four-year-olds can handle the whole process.

Make bread: Heat to lukewarm ½ c. milk. Remove from heat. Add 1 pkg. dry yeast. Stir in 1 tsp. salt and 1 tbsp. sugar. Stir in 2 to 2½ c. flour. Mix. Knead. Let rise 1 hr. over radiator. Bake in loaf pan 20 to 25 minutes.

Make butter: Use whipping cream at room temperature. Put in tight-fitting or screw-capped container and shake.

Make vegetable soup: Have each child bring a vegetable from home. Use bouillon cubes for stock and have a can of tomatoes on hand.

Make ice cream: Use hand freezer and place it inside plastic wading pool to keep melting ice and salt from floor.

Make Indian headbands from the top half of paper bags which were used for Halloween masks.

Make Indian beads: Use wet clay. Use toothpick to pierce beads. Paint with tempera when dry, and spray with acrylic.

Potato and vegetable printing.

Tissue-paper transparencies: With diluted Elmer's glue or pectin, stick vari-colored and varishaped pieces of colored tissue on manila paper. Wash over again with the diluted solution.

❈❈ 14 ❈❈
Now Comes Christmas
Planning for December

In the world of the three-, four-, and five-year-olds, Hanukkah, Santa Claus, and Christmas are the *now* of their days. If the local merchants can wait until after Thanksgiving for Santa Claus to be helicoptered in, we can be happy. The TV hawkers have already determined what toys the children will be wanting. All of the *want* pressure is on.

Parents of Jewish children will be glad to share information about their celebration with your children. Special cookies, candles, dreydls, and songs are things which they will share.

It is a very good idea to have a Santa Claus suit in the dress-up box at this time. The children play both the role of Santa Claus and also of his visitors. Careful listening will give you clues to feelings the child is having about himself. He really is feeling he is not *good enough.* A Santa may ask a visitor if she is nice to her little sister or he may ask one who has an eating problem, "Do you drink all your milk?" and so on. This acting out will give opportunities to us, if we listen, to do some positive teaching through our relationships during the month. The Santa Claus message that you have *to be good to get* has carried over into many an adult's thinking about God. Many churches never mention Santa Claus for fear that in some way disbelief will affect the Christmas story when the child begins to know about Santa Claus. However, since no child is isolated from the Santa Claus idea, we need to experience with him the positive aspects of the role. The personal identity book to use is *Alexander* by Harold Littledale (Parents' Magazine Press, 1964).

Another popular interest center during the month could be a large carton cave with straw strewn on the floor. A box manger, a baby doll, and a few scarves are all the props needed. If you have Jewish children, have some candle lighting.

Block figures of Mary, Joseph, baby, and animals are available from Community Playthings, Rifton, New York, or Freedom Crafts, Fredonia, Georgia. A Christmas tree should be set up two weeks before school is dismissed for the holidays. The tree can be decorated with coin holders which have been previously distributed. This program is sponsored by the American

Friends Service Committee, Philadelphia, and is called "Share Your Holiday with Children Around the World."

BOOKS

Anderson, Phoebe, *The First Christmas*. Philadelphia: United Church Press.

Brown, Margaret Wise, *Pussycat's Christmas*. New York: Thomas Y. Crowell Company, 1949.

Dutch version, *Jesus Is Born*. Minneapolis: Augsburg Publishing House, 1967.

Hemphill, Martha, *A Book About Jesus*. Valley Forge: Judson Press, 1969.

_____, *Christmas*. Valley Forge: Judson Press, 1969.

★Littledale, Harold, *Alexander*. New York: Parents' Magazine Press, 1964.

Shulz, Florence, *Jesus Was Born*. Philadelphia: United Church Press.

Welch, Jean-Louise, *The Animals Come First*. New York: Henry Z. Walck, Inc., 1963.

Woodard, Carol, *The Very Special Baby*. Philadelphia: Fortress Press, 1969.

FILMSTRIPS

Filmstrips which may be used:

Christmas with Carol and Peter, Society Visual Education, Chicago, Illinois

God Cares Through People, Family Filmstrips, Hollywood, California

The Little Engine That Could, Society Visual Education

The Little Pine Tree, Society Visual Education

Making Christmas Cookies, Jam Handy, Detroit, Michigan

Make Way for Ducklings, Weston Woods, Weston, Connecticut

Paddy's Christmas, Society Visual Education

SONGS

Songs which may be used include songs from denominational curriculum materials, folk songs, etc.

GRACE

Use chorus from "Rejoice, Ye Pure in Heart."

MOTOR PERCEPTUAL ACTIVITIES

Emphasize backward movements.

Stock exercises: Tap on floor, tap all the way around self, changing hands in back. Tap elbows, shoulders, and knees. Touch stick to elbow and floor, elbow and knee, elbow and toes, elbow and nose.

Draw a Christmas tree on floor with stick.

Put on Christmas balls with elbows.

Jump over stick frontwards and backwards.

ACTIVITIES

Field trip to church sanctuary just before the holidays to feel the beauty and to hear the organ play Christmas music.

Make Christmas cookies. Use any simple cut-out recipe.

Visit a shut-in or elderly person and sing some songs for them.

Make room decorations: Mobile using pine branch, door swags, or window-sill arrangements.

Make tree trimmings for home: String straws and squares. Make paper chains from duotone paper. Decorate metal-rimmed price tags with glitter. Cut paper spirals.

Make torn paper wreaths: Teacher tears out wreath shape from manila paper and children paste torn green paper bits on it and attach red crepe-paper bow.

Table decorations: Make cone-shaped Christmas trees by using cone-shaped drinking cups and covering with curled green paper strips. Strips are 3" x ½", curled with table knife. Glitter may also be sprinkled on and will adhere to the surplus rubber cement smeared on the cone. Green candy papers can be used on cone-shaped cups instead of curled papers. Use the large cone cups which are quite sturdy.

Christmas cards: Paste stars on wedge-shaped sections of paper doilies, and mount on card-shaped construction paper. Paste a green triangle on a card and decorate with paper reinforcement circles.

Paste torn bits of green paper within a triangular outline.

Paste curled green paper on a triangular outline.

Make a living Christmas tree: Cut tree shape from green blotting paper. Cover, using water-soluble paste, with rye grass seed. Stick a little tab on the back. The grass seed will sprout and grow indefinitely. Hang the tree on the outside of the glass with tab in the water. Keep glass filled with water.

Presents for parents: Handprints for threes. Use paper plates with picture hanger glued to the back. Put tempera paint in foil pan. Put child's hand in paint and print on plate.

Silhouettes for fours and fives. Use film strip projector for casting shadow on 12" x 18" white paper. Teacher should cut out shape which she outlined. Child mounts it on 12" x 18" black or dark blue paper.

Fingerpaint Christmas card holders. Use gallon ice cream containers. Fingerpaint with green directly on carton. When dry, decorate with stars and legal seals.

❦ 15 ❦
Wintertime Fun and Families
Planning for January

In those parts of the country where we have snow and ice, the emphasis will be on the season. In the places where children do not have these emphases, we focus on the family, homes, and family relationships. In small groups or in one-to-one relationships there can be many opportunities to talk out feelings about big or little brothers, mean daddies, unfair home treatment, fears, or whatever is bothering a child. One school had very successful small group conversations with the pastor in which the only ground rule was that only one person could talk at a time. Read the chapter on "Listening with Kindergarten Children" from Moustaka's *The Authentic Teacher* for examples of this type of a group.

BOOKS

Books which may be used in developing the winter seasonal theme:

Bancroft, Henrietta, and Van Gelder, Richard G., *Animals in Winter.* New York: Thomas Y. Crowell Company, 1963.

Beskow, Elsa M., *Pelle's New Suit.* Bronx, N.Y.: Platt & Munk, 1929.

Branley, Franklyn M., *Big Tracks, Little Tracks.* New York: Thomas Y. Crowell Company, 1960.

————, *Snow Is Falling.* New York: Thomas Y. Crowell Company, 1963.

Brown, Margaret Wise, *Winter Noisy Book.* New York: Harper & Row, Publishers, 1947.

Buckley, Helen E., *Josie and the Snow.* New York: Lothrop, Lee & Shepard Co., Inc., 1964.

Burton, Virginia L., *Katy and the Big Snowplow.* Boston: Houghton Mifflin Company.

Hader, Berta and Elmer, *The Big Snow.* New York: The Macmillan Company.

Kay, Helen, *One Mitten Lewis.* New York: Lothrop, Lee & Shepard Co., Inc., 1955.

Keats, Ezra Jack, *A Snowy Day.* New York: The Viking Press, Inc., 1962.

Kessler, Ethel, *The Day Daddy Stayed Home.* Garden City, N.Y.: Doubleday & Company, Inc.

Krauss, Ruth, *The Happy Day.* New York: Harper & Row, Publishers, 1949.

Lenski, Lois, *I Like Winter.* New York: Henry Z. Walck, Inc., 1950.

Lothrop, Dorothy P., *Who Goes There?* New York: The Macmillan Company.

Ozone, Lucy, *Surprise.* Skokie, Ill.: Rand McNally & Co.

Parker, B. M., *Winter Is Here.* New York: Harper & Row, Publishers, 1958.

Slobodkin, Florence, *Too Many Mittens*. Eau Claire, Wis.: E. M. Hale and Company, Pubs.

Tresselt, A., *White Snow, Bright Snow*. New York: Lothrop, Lee & Shepard Co., Inc.

Books for family or home emphasis:

Borack, Barbara, *Grandpa*. New York: Harper & Row, Publishers, 1967.

Brown, Myra B., *Amy and the New Baby*. New York: Franklin Watts, Inc., 1965.

Buckley, Helen E., *Grandfather and I*. New York: Lothrop, Lee & Shepard Co., Inc., 1959.

————, *Grandmother and I*. New York: Lothrop, Lee & Shepard Co., Inc.

Carton, Lonnie, *Daddies*. New York: Random House, Inc., 1963.

★Chaffin, Lillie D., *Tommy's Big Problem*. New York: Lantern Press, Inc., 1965.

Cooke, Barbara, *My Daddy and I*. New York: Abelard-Schuman Limited, 1961.

Green, M. M., *Everybody Has a House*. New York: William R. Scott, Inc., 1961.

★Holland, R., *A Bad Day*. New York: David McKay Co., Inc., 1964.

Krauss, Ruth, *The Big World and the Little House*. New York: Harper & Row, Publishers, 1956.

Lenski, Lois, *Big Little Davy*. New York: Henry Z. Walck, Inc., 1956.

★Locke, Edith Raymond, *The Red Door*. New York: Vanguard Press, Inc., 1965.

★Martin, Bill, *David Was Mad*. New York: Holt, Rinehart & Winston, Inc.

Miles, Betty, *A House for Everyone*. New York: Alfred A. Knopf, Inc., 1958.

Mizumura, Kazue, *If I Were a Mother*. New York: Thomas Y. Crowell Company, 1968.

Moore, the Harry Moore family, *The Sad Dad*. Valley Forge: Judson Press, 1969.

Parish, Peggy, *Willy Is My Brother*. Young Scott Books.

★Schlein, Miriam, *The Way Mothers Are*. Chicago: Albert Whitman & Co., 1963.

FILMSTRIPS AND MOVIES

Filmstrips which may be used:

All Kinds of Houses, Encyclopedia Britannica, Chicago, Illinois

Birthday Surprise for Daddy, Family Filmstrips, Hollywood, California

God Needs You to Care for Others, Family Filmstrips

Hercules, Weston Woods, Weston, Connecticut

Jesus and the Children, Family Filmstrips

Millions of Cats, Weston Woods

When Daddy Comes Home, Family Filmstrips

Winter, Encyclopedia Britannica

Movies to be rented:

Evans Corner, Contemporary Films, Evanston, Illinois

Ugly Duckling, Disney, University of Illinois, Audio Visual Library, Champaign, Illinois

MOTOR EXPLORATION

Begin work on balance: Stand on one foot. Use other foot to draw a snowman in the air.

Use big, little, fast, slow steps.

Hop across the room on one foot.

Encourage unusual ways of touching hands together.

Swing arms across the body slowly, fast.

Lean over and let arms swing of their own weight.

SONGS

Songs to be used for winter emphasis:

The children will enjoy "melting" in the sun.

> "Mitten Song"
> Thumb in the thumb place
> Fingers altogether
> This is the song we sing
> In mitten weather.

Activity Recording, "Winter Fun," Children's Record Guild, New York, New York.

Songs to be used for family emphasis from *Come Sing with Me,* Margaret Crain McNeil (Judson Press, 1972):
"Tell Me, Tell Me"
"In Our Family"
"My Home Is Where I Live"

FINGER PLAYS (Traditional) :

Five little snowmen
Knocking at my door,
One melted away,
And then there were four.

Four little snowmen
Looking at me,
One melted away,
And then there were three.

Three little snowmen
Looking at you,
One melted away,
And then there were two.

Two little snowmen
Playing in the sun,
One melted away,
And then there was one.

One little snowman
When the day was done
Melted away
And then there were none.

(Hold hand with fingers hanging downwards)

Five slick icicles hanging from the wall
This one says, "I'm very, very small!"
This one says, "I'm very, very tall!"
This one says, "Let's play, let's play!"
This one says, "Let's run away!"
This one says, "Burr! It's cold outside!"
Out came the sun and they melted away fast.
Isn't it too bad that the icicles can't last?

Dramatization using the "Outdoor Song."

An Outdoor Song

Geraldine Knarr

G. K.

1. It's fun to go wad-ing in sum-mer-time, In sum-mer-time, In sum-mer-time,
2. It's fun to make snow-men in win-ter-time, In win-ter-time, in win-ter-time,
3. It's fun to go walk-ing in spring-time rain, In spring-time rain, in spring-time rain,
4. It's fun to rake leaves in au-tumn time, In au-tumn time, in au-tumn time.

It's fun to go wad-ing in sum-mer-time. We have such fun to-geth-er.
It's fun to make snow-men in win-ter-time.
It's fun to go walk-ing in spring-time rain.
It's fun to rake leaves in au-tumn time.

It's fun to make snow angels, snowmen, big tracks, snowballs, to go skiing, etc. Have children choose the activity and sing the song. This can be used for all four seasons and children can guess the season from the activity being dramatized.

GAMES

"Did You Ever See A Lassie?"

Children show ways of helping.

Sing "Put Me Away" to the tune of "Frere Jacque."

Put many small articles in a pile in center of circle, such as blocks, crayons, small cars, scissors, etc. Sing:

> Here I am.
> Here I am.
> Where do I belong?
> Where do I belong?
> Please come and get me.
> Please come and get me.
> Put me away.
> Put me away.

(Children volunteer, one at a time, to put an article away until all are gone.)

ACTIVITIES

Easel painting: Use blue newsprint and black and white tempera.

Snow sculpture: Outdoors.

Squeeze-bottle painting: Use white tempera, colored paper.

Collages: Made of cotton, yarn, felt, rickrack, soda straws, cocktail picks.

Soap suds painting.

Frost pictures: Rubber cement on blue paper. Sprinkle with salt.

String painting.

White chalk on colored paper.

Snow pictures: Made by dissecting lace doilies to simulate snowflakes.

Bird feeders: Put wheat paste on sandpaper. Press wild bird seed into paste. Use yarn for handle for hanging.

Make dough balls of wheat paste, bird seed, suet, and corn. Let children grind suet and corn.

Use rolling pin and let children roll out bread crumbs.

Household chores: Let children wash windows, doll clothes, dishes, and let them scour tables.

Make a scrap bag! Use paper bag, and paste on following note:

Dear Mom and Dad,

Help me fill this sack with treasures for our scrap box. We can use small scraps of material, wood, rickrack, buttons, lace, bottle caps, nails, wood shavings, old playing cards, gift wrap, ribbons, string, feathers, cocktail picks, bits and odds of anything which you think we might use.

Thank you!

✿ 16 ✿
Helping Hearts and Hands
Planning for February

Valentine's Day is one of the big days in the young set's year. For this reason the activities of the first two weeks of February center around making valentines, decorating the room, and getting ready for a party. Beautiful mobiles can be made by painting a small branch white and hanging on it both snowflake shapes and hearts which the children have cut out. Be sure to send a list of the children's names home with each child. Many good home experiences result as conversation ensues from the choosing of this or that particular valentine for a child. The theme for emphasis for the month is "Community Helpers."

INTEREST CENTERS

Interest centers which may be used during the month are:

Doctor's waiting room: Chairs side by side, a small table with telephone, notepad, and pencil. Books on a rack close by.

Doctor's examination room: Cover table with a long strip of white paper fastened down with tape, stethoscope in evidence. Band-aids may be purchased in lots of 100 for one dollar at medical supply houses.

Barbershop: Wrap scissor blades with masking tape. See a local shave center for discarded shavers. Take off cord. Disposable paper gowns available from medical supply houses.

Beauty shop: Use a plastic mixing bowl and attach in some way to the back of a chair. Have rollers, combs, and mirror available.

Filling Station: Have plenty of large cartons available. A vacuum cleaner hose and a tire pump are good props.

FIELD TRIPS

To an animal hospital and a car wash. Invite a fireman to bring a truck to the parking lot of the school. He might explain the fire alarm system in your building or demonstrate the use of a fire extinguisher.

MOTOR EXPLORATION

Continue experimenting with balance, other than standing on one foot — try a one hand and one foot stand.

Experiment with sideways movements.

Toss sticks from one hand to another.

Use "Johnny Works with One Hammer," traditional kindergarten song, *This Is Music* (Allyn & Bacon, Inc.).

Find out about hips — find and feel by standing on one foot and swinging the other.

Wrap middle fingers and draw with each hand a heart shape on the floor.

Swing arms across the body.

Continue "tense and relax" exercise.

Raise walking beam 2 inches from floor; place a 2-inch cube on it for children to step over as they traverse the distance, focusing straight ahead.

Start hearing screening. Write Zenith Radio, Mooseheart, Illinois, about Moose program, or contact your local Moose Lodge for a detailed description of this program.

BOOKS

★Brown, Myra, *Casey's Sore-Throat Day*. New York: Franklin Watts, Inc.

Caldwell, John C., *Let's Visit* Series. New York: The John Day Company.

Chase, Francine, *A Visit to the Hospital*. New York: Grosset & Dunlap, Inc.

Flock, Marjorie, *Ask Mr. Bear*. New York: The Macmillan Company, 1932.

Garn, Bernard J., *A Visit to the Dentist*. New York: Grosset & Dunlap, Inc., 1959.

Greene, Carla, *I Want to Be* Books. Chicago: Childrens Press.

_____*Doctors and Nurses: What Do They Do?* New York: Harper & Row, Publishers, 1963.

Hoff, Syd, *Who Will Be My Friends?* New York: Harper & Row, Publishers, 1960.

Jubelier, Ruth, *About Jack's Dental Checkup*. Chicago: Childrens Press.

Katzwinkle, William, *Firemen*. New York: Pantheon Books, Inc., 1969.

Keats, Ezra J., *A Letter to Amy*. New York: Harper & Row, Publishers, 1968.

Kunhardt, Dorothy, *Gas Station Gus*. New York: Harper & Row, Publishers, 1961.

Lakritz, Esther, *Randy Visits the Doctor*. Nashville: Broadman Press, 1962.

Lenski, Lois, *Papa Small*. New York: Henry Z. Walck, Inc., 1951.

Puner, Helen, *Daddies and What They Do All Day*. New York: Lothrop, Lee & Shepard Co., Inc.

Pyne, Mabel, *The Hospital*. Boston: Houghton Mifflin Company, 1962.

Schlein, Miriam, *Amazing Mr. Pelgrew*. Eau Claire, Wis.: E. M. Hale and Company, Pubs., 1957.

★_____, *The Way Mothers Are*. Chicago: Albert Whitman & Co., 1963.

Seligman and Levine, *Tommy Visits the Doctor*. New York: Golden Press, Inc.

Smith, Robert P., *When I Am Big*. New York: Harper & Row, Publishers, 1965.

Watts, Robert A., *Who Are Billy's Friends?* Nashville: Broadman Press, 1964.

Wright, Ethel, *Saturday Walk*. New York: William R. Scott, Inc., 1954.

When reading the story *Ask Mr. Bear,* it is good to substitute the wording, "What can I give my mother for a valentine?" when Danny asks the question. In one school the teachers have facetiously subtitled *The Way Mothers Are* "Gospel for Modern Kitties."

There are many suppliers of good picture sets of community helpers. These are fairly traditional, and we need to find some showing women and also various racial backgrounds of community helpers. We need to do our part in getting mothers out of the kitchen as far as little children are concerned anyway. We perpetuate a good many stereotypes unknowingly.

FILMSTRIPS

Filmstrips may include:

Airplanes, Encyclopedia Britannica, Chicago, Illinois
A Letter to Amy, Weston Woods, Weston, Connecticut
The Fireman, Jam Handy, Detroit, Michigan
The Grocer, Jam Handy
The Mailman, Jam Handy
The Policeman, Jam Handy
Safety Helpers, Jam Handy

SONGS

"Love Somebody," *This Is Music* (Allyn & Bacon).
"What Are You Going to Be?" *This Is Music* (Allyn & Bacon).

GAME

"Postman Brings a Valentine," sing to the tune of "Mulberry Bush."

An old Cub Scout shirt makes a good postman's uniform.

The postman brings a valentine	*(Postman circles*
A valentine, a valentine	*around and chooses*
The postman brings a valentine	*someone to receive*
It says that I love you.	*the valentine.)*

FINGER PLAY: (Traditional)

One red valentine,
Two red valentines,
Three red valentines, four!
I cut and cut
And paste and paste
And then make twenty more.

BODY PLAY

"The Elevator Man," *New Songs and Games,* Ethel Crownin-shield (Boston: Boston Music Company).

"Clap Your Hands," Ruth Crawford Seeger (Doubleday & Company, Inc., 1948).

ACTIVITIES

Make valentines of all kinds.

Use red and white paint at easel.

Fingerpaint white and lift off on red paper cut into heart shapes.

Make individual mail bags out of paper sacks, size 16. Have each child decorate his own with potato print hearts. When the big day comes. the bags are opened and fastened to the edge of the counter or table by a length of masking tape. With help from the teacher each child mails his own. When children are down on their mats for resting, give each his bag to open his valentines. If you have a tape recorder, these moments are delightful to record the conversation and exclamations.

Field trip: Take a trip to the corner mailbox. First, make a valentine for mother and daddy. The envelopes need to be addressed ahead of time, but each child can affix his own stamp. Try to have the trip coincide with the pick-up time so that children can see their mail picked up and dumped into the big brown bag and then put in the red, white, and blue truck to be taken away.

Make hats: Mailman's, nurse's, doctor's, and fireman's.

❄❄ 17 ❄❄
Spring Is Coming
Planning for March

In most parts of the country, by March we begin to feel now that it will not be too long before new life will be appearing. In the parts of the country where we have winter there will still be many days of snow and cold ahead, but there will also be days in which we feel the touch of spring in the air. Some of the activities through which we can lead a child to wonder at this time are:

1. Scoop up a layer of dirt from outdoors, place in a cake pan, and bring inside. There will be many surprises as the dormant seeds in the dead grass start to grow.
2. Plant some of the wild birdseed in a cake pan and see what plants made the food which you served the winter birds.
3. Force branches of forsythia and other flowering shrubs by placing them in warm water.
4. Plant paper narcissus bulbs in gravel and water. Place in a dark place for one week to root. Take out and allow three weeks for Easter blooms.
5. Try planting seeds from citrus fruits, avocado seeds, pineapple tops, carrots, and sweet potatoes.
6. Make a cage for cocoons by using a cake pan top and bottom separated by hardware cloth. Cloth fits into pans and overlaps itself for closure. Take cocoons out of refrigerator (stored there since fall), sprinkle with water, and place in cage to hatch.

BOOKS

Books which may be used in group time or individually:

★Brown, Margaret Wise, *The Dead Bird*. New York: William R. Scott, Inc., 1958.

Duvoisin, Roger, *Day and Night*. New York: Alfred A. Knopf, Inc., 1959.

Ets, Marie H., *Gilberto and the Wind*. New York: The Viking Press, Inc., 1963.

Flack, Marjorie, *Wait for William*. Boston: Houghton Mifflin Company.

Goldin, Augusta, *Straight Hair, Curly Hair*. New York: Thomas Y. Crowell Company, 1966.

Guilfaile, E., *Nobody Listens to Andrew*. Chicago: Follett Publishing Company.

Hall, Adelaide, *The Rain Puddle*. New York: Lothrop, Lee & Shepard Co., Inc., 1965.

★Hitte, Kathryn, *Boy, Was I Mad!* New York: Parents' Magazine Press, 1969.

★Johnston, Johanna, *Edie Changes Her Mind*. New York: G. P. Putnam's Sons, 1964.

Kauffman, Lois, *What's That Noise?* New York: Lothrop, Lee & Shepard Co., Inc., 1965.

Klein, Leonore, *Mud, Mud, Mud*. New York: Alfred A. Knopf, Inc., 1962.

Klimowicz, Barbara, *Fred, Fred, Use Your Head*. Nashville: Abingdon Press.

Kuskin, Karla, *James and the Rain*. New York: Harper & Row, Publishers, 1957.

Ozone, Lucy, *All in One Day*. Chicago: Albert Whitman & Co., 1955.

★Sendak, Maurice, *Where the Wild Things Are*. New York: Harper & Row, Publishers, 1963.

————, *A Baby Starts to Grow*. New York: Thomas Y. Crowell Company, 1965.

Showers, Paul, *Your Skin and Mine*. New York: Thomas Y. Crowell Company, 1965.

Simon, Norma, *The Wet World*. Philadelphia: J. B. Lippincott Co.

Udraz, J. M., *Mary Ann's Mud Day*. New York: Harper & Row, Publishers.

★Viorst, Judith, *I'll Fix Anthony*. New York: Harper & Row, Publishers, 1969.

Zolotow, Charlotte, *The Sleepy Book*. New York: Lothrop, Lee & Shepard Co., Inc. 1958.

————, *The Storm Book*. New York: Harper & Row, Publishers.

FILMSTRIPS AND MOVIES

Animals in Spring, Encyclopedia Britannica, Chicago, Illinois
Birds Grow, Jam Handy, Detroit, Michigan
Cows on the Farm, Jam Handy
How Butterflies Grow, Jam Handy
Mr. and Mrs. Robin's Springtime Family, Society Visual Education, Chicago, Illinois
People in Spring, Encyclopedia Britannica
Pigs on the Farm, Jam Handy
Playing in the Rain, Family Filmstrips, Hollywood, California
Sandbox and Trike, Family Filmstrips
Spring, Encyclopedia Britannica
Terri's Turtle, Jam Handy
What Is Wind? Jam Handy

Movies available from Three Prong, New York, New York:

"Me Too Show" series
Water Is Wet
If I Were an Animal

MOTOR EXPLORATION

Raise walking board two inches. Children walk backwards, looking straight ahead.

Running.

Painting full-size outline of themselves.

Making caterpillar movements.

Running, stopping on cue.

Field trip to YMCA for trampoline usage.

SONGS

"It's a Small World," Disney

"Sing a Song of Gladness," *Martin and Judy Songs,* compiled by Edith Lovell Thomas (Beacon Press).

Songs from *Come Sing with Me,* Margaret Crain McNeil (Judson Press, 1972) :

"Look, Oh, Look!"

"Grow Little Seeds"

ACTIVITIES

Make kazoos out of toilet paper tubes. Cover one end with tissue, and secure with rubber band. Have children decorate with felt markers and make *"oo"* wind sound through it.

Cut crepe-paper wind streamers for outdoor play.

Fashion a paper-bag kite by attaching string to one of the open ends. May decorate. Children run against the wind with these.

Use water play inside.

Blow soap bubbles.

Make butterflies using squeeze-bottle techniques.

Offer children staplers and pieces of cardboard for experimentation.

New Life Outdoors
Planning for April

In April the entire focus will be on new life and outdoor experiences.

BOOKS

Books which may be used for resources follow:

Brawley, Eleanor R., *Lisa's Spring Baby*. Richmond, Va.: John Knox Press, 1969.

Clymer, Eleanor, *Belinda's New Spring Hat*. New York: Franklin Watts, Inc., 1969.

Downer, Mary Louise, *The Flower*. New York: William R. Scott, Inc., 1955.

Fine, Aaron, *Peter Plants a Pocketful*. Eau Claire, Wis.: E. M. Hale and Company, Pubs.

Flack, Marjorie, *Tim Tadpole and the Great Bullfrog*. Garden City, N.Y.: Doubleday & Company, Inc., 1959.

Friskey, Margaret, *Johnny and the Monarch*. Chicago: Childrens Press, 1961.

Fritz, Jean, *Bunny Hopwell's First Spring*. New York: Wonder Books, Inc.

Gay, Zhenya, *The Nicest Time of the Year*. New York: The Viking Press, Inc., 1960.

Grant, Bruce, *How Chicks Are Born*. Skokie, Ill.: Rand McNally & Co.

Hawkinson, Lucy, *Days I Like*. Chicago: Albert Whitman & Co., 1965.

Holl, Adelaide, *The Remarkable Egg*. New York: Lothrop, Lee & Shepard Co., Inc., 1968.

Krauss, Ruth, *The Carrot Seed*. New York: Harper & Row, Publishers, 1945.

Lenski, Lois, *Spring Is Here*. New York: Henry Z. Walck, Inc., 1945.

Martin, Bill and Bernard, *The Little Squeegy Bug*. New York: Holt, Rinehart & Winston, Inc., 1945.

Pohl, Louis, *It's Really Nice*. Boston: Little, Brown and Company, 1960.

Tresselt, Alvin, *Hi, Mr. Robin*. New York: Lothrop, Lee & Shepard Co., Inc., 1950.

Udry, Janice May, *A Tree Is Nice*. New York: Harper & Row, Publishers, 1956.

Walker, Herbert, *A Moth Is Born*. Skokie, Ill.: Rand McNally & Co.

FILMSTRIPS

Mary's Easter Lambs, Society Visual Education, Chicago, Illinois
Mrs. Hen's Easter Surprise, Society Visual Education
Rackety Rabbit, Society Visual Education
Surprise, Family Filmstrips, Hollywood, California

MOTOR EXPLORATION

Run hard, stop on cue, feel heart beating.
Roll.

Jump zigzag over rope stretched flat on floor.

Lie on floor on back and have feet be windshield wipers.

FIELD TRIPS

To greenhouses, to farms to see baby lambs, to hatcheries to see baby chicks, and to a farm to see sheep shearing.

SONGS

From *Come Sing with Me,* Margaret Crain McNeil (Judson Press, 1972):

"Weather Song"

"The Seasons"

Song of the Seed, Cecile Lamb (Standard Publishing).

GAME

Oats, Peas, Beans, and Barley Grow

ACTIVITIES

Make fondant Easter eggs. Mix powdered sugar, milk, vanilla, and food coloring. Give each child a ball to knead and make his own jelly-bean-sized eggs.

Gadget printing.

Sponge painting, use light tapping touch.

Roller painting, using brayers.

Swab-stick painting.

Colored chalk drawing on manila paper. Fix with liquid starch.

Plant seeds in peat pots for Mother's Day gift. Nasturtiums, dwarf variety, grow quickly and should be ready for that day.

❦❦ 19 ❦❦
The Year Is Ending
Planning for May

Continue to use the outdoors as much as possible in May, taking walks and using the playground for digging and water play. Using big wide brushes to paint the outside of the building with water is fascinating as is blueprinting some of the specimens found growing along the alleys or in the churchyard. We call these blueprints sun pictures. Shadow play is fun and so is hoop rolling and jumping rope. If there is a nearby area for picnics, the children can prepare their own sack lunches at school before the excursion.

Other emphases this month are on concepts: over and under, big and small, hard and easy; the senses; math concepts; and colors.

BOOKS

Aliki, *My Five Senses*. New York: Thomas Y. Crowell, 1965.

Berger, Terry, *I Have Feelings*. New York: Behavioral Publications, Inc., 1971.

Berkley, Ethel, *Big, Little, Up and Down*. Young Scott Books.

Brown, Margaret Wise, *The Color Kittens*. Racine, Wis.: Golden Press, Inc.

_____, *The Quiet Noisy Book*. New York: Harper & Row, Publishers, 1950.

Friskey, Margaret, *Chicken Little Count to Ten*. Chicago: Childrens Press.

Garelick, May, *Sounds of a Summer's Night*. New York: William R. Scott, Inc., 1954.

_____, *What's Inside?* New York: William R. Scott, Inc., 1955.

Gibson, Myra T., *What Is Your Favorite Smell, My Dear?* New York: Grossett & Dunlap, Inc., 1964.

_____, *What Is Your Favorite Thing to Hear?* New York: Grossett & Dunlap, Inc., 1966.

_____, *What Is Your Favorite Thing to Touch?* New York: Grossett & Dunlap, Inc.

Jean, Priscilla, *Patty Round and Wally Square*. New York: Ivan Obelensky, Inc.

Kaufman, Joe, *Big and Little*. Racine, Wis.: Golden Press, Inc., 1966.

Kessler, Ethel, *Are You Square?* Garden City, N.Y.: Doubleday & Company, Inc.

Kohn, Bernice, *Everything Has a Shape and Everything Has a Size*. Englewood Cliffs, N.J.: Prentice-Hall, Inc., 1966.

Schlein, Miriam, *Shapes*. New York: William R. Scott, Inc., 1952.

Schneider, Herman and Nina, *How Big Is Big?* Eau Claire, Wis.: E. M. Hale and Company, Pubs.

Scott, Rochelle, *Colors, Colors All Around.* New York: Grossett & Dunlap, Inc.

Selsam, Millicent, *All About Eggs.* New York: William R. Scott, Inc., 1952.

Shopp, Martha and Charles, *Let's Find Out About Wheels.* New York: Franklin Watts, Inc.

Showers, Paul, *Find Out by Touching.* New York: Thomas Y. Crowell Company, 1961.

_____, *The Listening Walk.* New York: Thomas Y. Crowell Company, 1961.

Walliser, Blair, *The Where's That? Book.* New York: Grossett & Dunlap, Inc., 1964.

Webber, Helen, *What Is Sour? What Is Sweet?* New York: Holt, Rinehart & Winston, Inc.

Webber, Irma, *Up Above and Down Below.* New York: William R. Scott, Inc., 1943.

Wilkin, Esther, *Baby Listens.* Racine, Wis.: Golden Press, Inc.

Witte, Eve and Pat, *The Touch Me Book.* Racine, Wis.: Golden Press, Inc., 1961.

Zoffo, George, *The Big Book of Real Boats and Ships.* New York: Grossett & Dunlap, Inc.

_____, *The Big Book of Real Trains.* New York: Grossett & Dunlap, Inc., 1963.

_____, *All the Colors.* New York: Grossett & Dunlap, Inc., 1964.

FILMSTRIPS

Going to the Country, Encyclopedia Britannica, Chicago, Illinois
Little Toot, Encyclopedia Britannica
Picnic in the Country, Family Filmstrips, Hollywood, California

SONGS

"Everybody," *Martin & Judy Songs* (Beacon Press).

Songs from *Come Sing with Me,* Margaret Crain McNeil (Judson Press, 1972):

"God Gave Me Eyes"
"I Am Glad I Have a Nose"
"I Feel Sad Inside"

MOTOR EXPLORATION

Opportunities for feeling and listening:

Moving toward a source of sound with eyes shut.
Creative acting out of corn popping.
Walking up ramp and jumping off.
Walking a beam, carrying a glass of water.
Doing simple puzzles with eyes closed.
With feet still, finding ways you can move your body.
Using balance board.

ACTIVITIES

Texture collages: Use nature materials—bark, sticks, grasses.

Gravel pictures.

Use shapes, squares, circles, triangles, and rectangles, and see what children do with them.

Make a feely bag for children to "see" with their fingers: This can be done by placing different objects in a plain brown bag; the children can then reach into the bag and identify the objects by their "feel." Some teachers use a box with holes in it. Another variation is to have children choose from the bag or box two objects which feel the same rather than have them identify the objects.

Make a smelling tray: Use box top and plastic pill bottles filled with scents and odors.

Make a tasting tray—sweet and sour.

Make mud paintings. Sift soil to get rid of sticks, and mix sifted soil with liquid starch. Finger paint on trays with this.

Chocolate pudding painting—fingerpaint directly on table top. Use instant variety.

Total experience—taste, smell, touch, and see.

Make blueprints.

Make wrapping paper for peat-potted plants.

Make Mother's Day card.

Use medicine droppers and shiny, coated paper for a new painting effect.

Use easel painting outside.

Have final conferences with parents during last weeks of school and enroll children for following year.

✿✿ 20 ✿✿
To What End?
Evaluating Our Successes and Failures

Most funding agencies require that you have an evaluation instrument to measure the success of your venture. Whether you benefit from outside funding or not, there should be every effort made to evaluate your entire ministry with young children.

Teachers should be growing in ways which help them personally, in the areas of communication and relationships, not only with children but with one another and with the parents. Continuous leadership training at all levels for your teachers should be provided for in the budget.

If your community has a 4C's program (Community Coordinated Child Care), your church should participate in it. Certainly anything which affects child care in your community should be part of the church's concern. Staff members of agencies specializing in particular areas, such as mental health, should be available to you for consultation.

Develop criteria for evaluating the child's growth in his relationships with others. These criteria might fall into the following general categories: interest, contacts, behavior, feelings, relationships with others, roles taken in play, special problems or trends, and evidences of growth in self-concepts and relationships. A good source book for help in developing criteria is *Observing and Recording the Behavior of Young Children* by Dorothy H. Cohen and V. Stern (Teachers College Press, Columbia University). This type of measurement should be done each month. It is amazing how much better one sees and feels about a child when one knows that the experiences will be evaluated in this way.

Whatever plans you may have for reporting to parents will be more effective if you have such a device for measurement. Each child being served should have his own file. It should contain the personal history form which the parents filled out on enrollment, the health form, and the blanket permission slip. The file should also contain behavior pattern records and the teacher's daily anecdotal records. During class time each teacher keeps a writing pad close at hand where she can jot down anything that happens which she thinks is significant. At the close of each session her notes are filed, and both she and the director have a good profile of the child when the time for parent conferences comes. These are confidential files only as far as other parents are concerned. There should be no withholding of any material from a child's parents.

Examples of daily records of two boys, Jeff and Tom, follow. They are four-year-olds with no particular problems or difficulties; hence the records are sparse. (Some files bulge.) These two boys were chosen because their backgrounds are similar. Their fathers are both professional men. Jeff has three older sisters, and Tom has one younger sister. The family structure is different, but the families have the same value system for their lives in the church and in the community.

TOM

9/23 Tom showed group how to do obstacle course—did everything well. Knocked stick off, tried again, and did OK. Went under stick with exact minimum of clearance.

9/28 Tommy came up to me smiling and said, "I made a new friend! Chad!" He beamed.

10/ 9 A few boys were playing roughly with a plastic ball—more like football play. Tom ran and slid right into two boys, then continued to play. He wrestled, ran, and fell—all of it—right with them. This went on for about half an hour. We had group time and Tom was still punching and poking at Greg to tussle again. He is sweaty and very red in the face. First we have seen this behavior from him. He looks as if he is enjoying it.

10/12 Tom joined in boys' wrestling and tumbling again. Seemed to promote it. All smiles while doing it. Participates well in all activities.

10/14 Tom asked to play with plastic ball. He and several boys really played with it, like touch football. At time to go, Tom just sat while waiting for his car, just sat looking exhausted, well-pleased expression, hair wet with sweat.

10/26 Tom tried to instigate fighting in room by charging Greg and Steve. Miss Karen asked him to wait until we were outside. He said, "OK," and then tackled Greg. He was smiling as he did this. Outside he and several boys rolled the barrel around and around. He became red and sweaty.

10/27 Tommy was the first and for a time the only one in his group to sing the Halloween songs.

11/ 3 Tom is still trying to instigate fighting. He charges with hands out repeatedly. Today in scuffle he got his head hit. Jim said, "He hit me so I hit him!" Tom cried and cried.

11/ 9 Tommy seemed distant today. On outside looking in. He did help shake cream for butter, but somehow seemed not with us.

1/ 8 Tommy built a great doghouse. Greg started to help but left. Tom finished. Made a walkie-talkie at the workbench. Tackled Steve at group time, ready to wrestle. I asked him to sit down and he did.

2/ 1 Played entire one and one-half hours in a very rough football game. Took a lot of knocks. Is the smallest boy in the group. Refused to move from the area except to run up to David when he came in to invite him to join in. David refused.

2/22 Tom enters the roughest play—but can still find a spot in a story group or a quiet project. His face shows happiness and real pleasure. He carries no noticeable hostility. He is well-rounded in all areas.

4/23 Tom, a quiet, shy child, went to rough-and-tumble to even keel, all in one year. Delightful child. Eager, enthusiastic—a thinker. Mom came today. Birthday. Five years old. He is happy! Very confident with others. Can take it and hand it out.

JEFF

9/23 Jeff did a lot of wandering on the obstacle course. Rolled OK.

9/24 Jeff painted at the easel very deliberately, multi-colored stripes. Sat at table, head resting in cupped hand, while working a puzzle—the fire engine one—very difficult. Never asked for help. Worked a long time. Very pleased with himself when he finished.

9/25 Jeff looked concerned, said his dad was in California and would be home for breakfast. He painted a beautiful painting. I asked if we could keep it and he said, "No." Every once in a while he asked if we were sure it was all right.

9/27 Jeff paints again and asks if we like it. He comments, "I always make nice pictures, don't I?" Standing on watch tower outside, sort of staring, says, "My dad is still in California but he's coming home to dinner." Asks for some help to come down the pole. Smiles when he gets down. Later, inside he plays in housekeeping corner and still later he rides the fire truck.

10/ 6 Jeff wanted to saw. Finally got a turn. Couldn't get saw to stay in one place. Chad started a groove for him. He worked and worked—couldn't cut the mustard! He quit. At going-home time questioned Miss Karen about his picture, "Was it nice?"

10/16 Played autoharp with Miss Karen. Seemed to have a perfect timing sense. On walk outside he sang, "Raindrops, falling on my head!"

10/18 Joined in building with blocks, then pulled out by himself, and built an airplane structure with wings, even a seat. Sat in it, pretended flying, verbal motor. Later got a long block and stuck it in one side. Said he was filling it with gas. Cut out his squirrel perfectly.

10/26 Jeff had laryngitis and a very bad cough. At easel his painting was sloppy in comparison with his usual exactness. He is unwilling to take off his own coat or put it on the hanger. I held it for him at outdoor time since he was the last one without a coat on. He put both arms in backward. I zipped it up. He said, "It's on backwards." Took it off himself and put it on himself. Outdoors he wanted to swing on the rope swing. He couldn't get the hang or accomplish sitting on the small board without falling off. He has good control of small muscles but not so good on large.

10/29 Guinea pigs were screaming loudly. Jeff was pinching them. Miss Karen said, "Jeff!" He quickly stopped and said, "I'm sorry; I didn't know I was hurting them." He went over and petted them again. Several times he repeated the pinching and when they squealed, he looked up to see if we were watching. At time to go home Michelle was in the cart. He sat on her and bounced up and down. She cried, "Get up! Get up!" He continued and I asked him to get up. He said, "I'm sorry; I didn't know I was hurting her." Earlier in the day Jeff was not able to make a Halloween mask. He cut two of them all up and seemed frustrated. A change in picture of him. Did a beautiful pumpkin painting at the easel.

11 /2 Jeff in motor exploratory group time. With it! Does everything.

11/ 3 Was very slow in making Indian headband. Did a beautiful design on it. Still refuses to put coat on. We sent him down to car without it on. While doing Visit to My Friend, he would poke at the guinea pigs each time he went by.

11/ 9 Repeatedly poked at guinea pigs. I laid his coat down upside down and showed him how he could put it on like "magic." He tried it twice.

11/11 Jeff hung his coat up today and when it was time to go outdoors, he put it on as he was shown. He beamed, "I did it, teacher!" He is very proud of something which he can do by himself.

As you can see by these notes on Jeff, it was time for a parent conference. Having three older sisters and having a daddy who was gone a great deal were really bad news for Jeff. In spite of this, the following note was received when we asked the mother to come in. "I will be in Washington, D.C., all this week and thus unable to come in for a coffee and room visitation. May I be rescheduled?" Things finally did get better for Jeff when everyone realized how much he was hurting.

Another type of evaluation is one made of a single session's activities. The following evaluation was made of an exploratory movement group on the playground, the week of May 17.

Children were able to detect some subtle differences in textures. Because the Wednesday group had grimy hands, and because we wanted to protect the textured cloth feely equipment, we used a simple form board and puzzles with single pieces. The children did these with eyes shut.
Billy had a very difficult time with this tactile problem.
Dave also had trouble.
Stephen felt carefully around the edges of the puzzle pieces and around the edges of the hole; successful.
Frank struggled and left the rectangle crosswise in its spot.
Bean-bag activity was more successful. More experimentation and less wild throwing.

This activity was good for only a few moments.
Added walking on the two-by-four with bean bag on head.
Most children able to tip the balance board.
Scott very shaky on two-by-four raised about a foot from ground.
Mark marks time on stairs, shaky about height.
Joy and Stacy have good balance.
Susan climbs over triangular ladders with fear and trembling but does it.
Nancy was asked to follow moving tambourine, walking, eyes shut. She was noticeably confused but did locate the sound and was able to follow until it turned. Then she lost it again.

Ministry with young children during the week is a demanding calling. This work requires qualities of steadfastness, unselfishness, self-denial, and servanthood, with lots of plain, hard, physical labor and drudgery. Let no one deceive himself as to the easiness of this task nor as to the financial rewards of this service. The boot struggle, the cleaning-up process, and the meager paycheck all attest to this fact.

Yet ministry with young children is a rewarding calling. Ministry *with*, not ministry *to*, young children means you are a very privileged person. You are a whole person involved in this ministry — not just the part of you which tells a story or plans an activity. Your head, your heart, your hands, your lap (it never is big enough), your knees (what they take!), your eyes, your ears, and your good strong back are all in the action. And interacting with all of you is each child — the whole child — whole in the complete sense also, not just the part that listens or responds to a direction. Wondering with young children is akin to worship, an experience which leads to a feeling of being on holy ground. The sharing in the hush of silence, the whisper of wondering words is worth the meager paycheck or a dozen pep pills. You are privileged because you share in the children's frankness, their openness. It is like new wine. Their discoveries of beauty in plain things are like sight restored; their awareness of their surroundings and of each other is like rebirth. You see, hear, and feel anew as you live with young children.

DATE DUE

SEP 27 1974		
FEB 12 '81		
SE 16'94		
OC 15'94		
DE 14 '01		

DEMCO 38-297